WOODEN TOYS

ALSO BY THE AUTHOR:

A Beginner's Book of Knitting and Crocheting
A Beginner's Book of Needlepoint and Embroidery
A Beginner's Book of Off-Loom Weaving
Creative Handweaving
Designing for Crafts
Hooked Rugs and Ryas
Mosaics in Needlepoint
Working in Leather

Submarine designed and made by Scott Chase Parker; Tiny Village houses designed and made by THE AMAZING RANDY; Rocking Horse pattern, Jointed Bear, Shaped-Outline Jigsaw Puzzle, Dachshund, Balancing Dancer, and Woodpecker designed and made by George O. Smith.

Photographs of the Submarine, Seaplane, Bus, Jointed Bear, Whimmy Diddle, Dump Truck, and Steam Tractor are by Scott Chase Parker.

WOODEN TOYS

Copyright © 1978 by Xenia Ley Parker. Copyright under International and Pan-American Copyright Conventions. All rights reserved, including the right to reproduce this book or portions thereof in any form, except for the inclusion of brief quotations in a review. All inquiries should be addressed to Hawthorn Books, Inc., 260 Madison Avenue, New York, New York 10016. This book was manufactured in the United States of America and published simultaneously in Canada by Prentice-Hall of Canada, Limited, 1870 Birchmount Road, Scarborough, Ontario.

Library of Congress Catalog Card Number: 77–92312

ISBN: 0–8015–4809–8

1 2 3 4 5 6 7 8 9 10

WOODEN TOYS

Xenia Ley Parker

HAWTHORN BOOKS, INC.
Publishers/New York
A Howard & Wyndham Company

For Chris

Contents

WOODEN
TOYS

Introduction

Wooden toys have a fascination that is felt by people of all ages. As plastic seems to surround us, the timeless beauty of natural wood is all the more appealing. Durable, attractive, and fun to make, these toys represent an ideal expression of useful creativity.

You can achieve the results you want by using the most basic hand tools and wood; and they can be bought at minimal expense. Even if you've never worked with wood, you can make all of the toys in this book. Before you know it, you'll be a seasoned woodworker, turning out toys that will be treasured for years to come.

All of the toys in this book can be made by a beginner. You will find that the number of parts in a toy is a good indication of its complexity. So even if you are a novice, you can select a basic toy right away and start applying your new skills as you learn by doing. Whether you want to make wooden toys for your own children, to give as prized gifts, to keep as sculptural forms, for sale as functional craft objects or for fund-raising activities, you'll find the simple construction techniques a pleasure.

Let's get started. The world of wooden toys is waiting.

1
Toys of Wood

Wood was no doubt one of the first materials to be made into useful objects in prehistoric times. It was readily available in most areas, and because it was easy to fashion, was used long before metal implements. When children of those days picked up a stick or two and used their imaginations to play a game, the first toys were created. As games and play became more sophisticated, each type of toy evolved into specific shapes with greater definition. Wooden toys have been with us ever since.

The toys with which we are the most familiar are quite similar to those of ages past. Dolls, hobby horses, games of skill, to name a few, were all known in ancient times. As civilization went on, toys developed along with technology. Many different materials became available and were employed to augment and decorate basic toys of wood.

Playthings of remarkable intricacy, made for fledgling pharaohs of ancient Egypt, seem more like art treasures than toys. The actual appearance of these, and toys from other parts of the world, is shown in frescoes, paintings, ceramics, and other works that preserve a record of daily life. Although these works usually depict the upper classes of any society, they are representative of the toys that were found in all homes. Actual examples of many toys have also been unearthed by archaeologists and can be seen in natural history, folk art, and fine art museums.

Toys made out of wood were prevalent wherever wood was found in abundance. As time went on and people began to have more specialized occupations, carpenters were often the toymakers. In the south of Germany in the late Middle Ages, toymakers guilds sprang up as the carvers of wood became the first to develop the art as a separate enterprise. Up until then, it was usually relegated to the off-hours of woodworkers or the sparse leisure time of parents. Bright, glossy enamels were used to paint these toys in the style of Bavaria. As they were exported to many parts of the globe, these designs continue to have an influence on the folk arts and toys of many countries.

In colonial America, the few imports that arrived just couldn't go around. To meet the needs of daily life, people gained self-sufficiency in all areas. They learned to "use it up, wear it out, make it do, or do without," as one of the popular sayings of the day went. Under the harsh light of Puritan standards, the ornate toys from Europe were inappropriate in any case. The earliest toys of settlers' children were severely limited in scope and number. Those that did exist would teach children something about their tasks and future roles. Instructional toys of wood, such as dolls, cradles, building blocks, and toy rifles were found acceptable to even the strictest families. During the long winter months, when little outdoor work could be done, toys were made. As time went on, toys would also amuse and entertain—the jointed dancing figure, which makes bouncing movements on a paddle, is still a crowd pleaser. In parts of rural America today, colonial-style toys are made in much the same manner as they were three hundred years ago. With the recent revival of interest in this period, these toys have regained a measure of widespread popularity.

Today, wooden toys in all kinds of shapes and sizes are seen. Fantastic animal forms coexist with basic puzzles and tops. Some of the new toymakers are professionals, who sell their works at craft fairs and toy shops. Most are part-timers, whose main vocation lies elsewhere, who enjoy the creation of sturdy, safe, attractive toys for family and friends.

Woodworking is sometimes thought to have a mystique which excludes the uninitiated who don't possess extensive workshops or a comprehension of intricate blueprint-like plans. Yet, nothing could be further from the truth. For wooden toys, all you need is to follow simple, effective construction methods with easily used hand tools. Anyone who wants to make wooden toys can—the main requirement is the desire to do so. You'll be surprised and pleased with the results of your first adventure in toy making. Your main problem will then become deciding which project to do next, as all kinds of ideas for toys will come to you.

2
What You'll Need to Know about Wood

Wood has always enjoyed special popularity as a medium of creativity because it lends itself so well to many kinds of craftwork. Its natural grain, inner glow, and unique textures are quite unlike anything else. The qualities of all types of wood are such that you'll discover that even the most basic constructions have great appeal.

Wood is, obviously, obtained from trees. Each type, or species, of tree has its own characteristics, formed as the tree grows. The grain, or cellular structure, is the name given to the textural makeup of a piece of wood. As the tree stands, the cells run in an up and down direction. The groups of growing cells carry water and nutrients from the soil up through their long, narrow, tubelike formations to the leaves and branches. Each tree grows in diameter around the center. This innermost section, called the pith, remains the same as layers of cells pile up around it. These layers are called annual rings because they form year by year.

When you look at a cross section of a tree trunk, you can clearly see the annual rings. Each is comprised of a wider, paler ring and a darker, more sharply defined second ring. These two parts make up one ring. The paler part occurs as the tree grows rapidly, with lots of available water, in the spring. These open-looking cells are followed by the denser late summer ring. As there is less moisture, the tree grows more slowly and the cells form closer together. In late fall and winter, trees rest. The cycle starts again in the spring as the tree resumes active growth.

As the years go on, the outermost layer of wood cells adds to itself and becomes farther removed from the inner pith. The outer layer is called the sapwood as it carries the sap that nourishes the tree. The older layers of sapwood become inner, inactive heartwood. The sapwood remains right next to the bark throughout the life of a tree; it is the heartwood that increases in width. A tree cannot continue to grow if the sapwood is extensively damaged, even if the heartwood is untouched and the tree is still standing.

The cambium layer is found between the sapwood and the bark. It creates the new layers of sapwood and it also adds to the density of the bark, which is like a protective outer wrapper. The medullary rays are groups of tightly packed cells which form at right angles to the annual rings, running from the pith out to the cambium layer.

As a tree grows in outward and upward layers, the existing annual rings change very little. If a foreign substance, such as a nail, were driven completely into a tree, it would stay in the same position, as compared to the height from the ground and the annual rings, as the tree continued to grow. Surprisingly, it would not move up or out as the tree grew taller and wider.

Mature trees are cut for lumber, usually during the dormant, cold winter period. In modern woodcutting, the forests are generally planned and managed so that there is always a new supply of wood growing to replace that which is removed. Each tree to be cut is selected and marked before any cutting actually takes place. The old, wasteful way of clear cutting, or razing an entire area, is rarely used unless the land is being leveled out for another purpose, such as farming.

Cut logs are brought to lumber mills, usually along a watery path. The wood is then sorted according to intended use. The most attractive parts of each tree, where the cells grow most closely together and the grain is finest, are found at what are known as the crotches. These are the joinings of trunk and branches where the additional strength of dense cell groupings is needed to hold the parts without pulling away from each other. Burl wood is of unusual beauty but fairly rare. Burls form as buds that would ordinarily protrude through the bark and become branches but which remain just under it. The bud continues to grow in densely convoluted form, creating a fascinating grain which is usually obtained at great expense.

The logs usually remain in the water, soaking as they are sorted and checked for burls and the like. There are several ways in which the wood is then cut at the mill, depending on the quality and characteristics of the logs. The soaking helps to season the wood. Seasoning is the treating of wood, in many steps, so that the finished lumber doesn't crack or split. Wood that has not been seasoned correctly will often come apart along its grain when it is worked or subjected to climate changes. That's one of the reasons why it is usually worth it to pay a little more and get good quality wood for your projects.

At the mill, very large band saws, whose blades are a continuous circle of cutting edge, cut up the logs into planks. In what is known as plain-sawing, the wood is cut from one end to the other in the desired thickness as many times as possible for each log. Quarter-cut wood is made by cutting a log into four sections before forming the planks. Then, each quarter is cut from one end to the other. These planks are formed at parallels to the medullary rays, perpendicular to the rings. This creates an interesting grain as the rays mark each plank. There is less wood produced from each quarter than might be in standard plain-sawing, but the enhanced grain qualities are felt to be worth the added wastefulness in cases where the grain is particularly important. Quarter-cut wood is naturally more expensive than the same type of wood cut in standard planks.

After cutting and trimming, the planks are stacked into layers. Each layer is separated from the next by an air space, so that the wood can be seasoned or cured. The spaces let air circulate and allow water to evaporate or drain out. The stacks of wood can be left for weeks, months, even years, according to the thickness and quality of the lumber. If you've ever seen a lumberyard, you've seen the huge stacks of ageing wood. After this step, the wood is then dried in a kiln or oven. The final drying can also take weeks to complete. All of these steps in curing the wood are essential, so that the finished planks don't crack, expand or contract unevenly, or bend out of shape.

The seasoned planks are often cut into shorter lengths for sale. At this time, a process called planing is also usually done. The wood is fed into large planers which shave off the required amount to create planks of uniform squareness and thickness. For the very rarest woods, each plank is cut into extremely thin layers known as veneers. These are then applied to other woods of lesser expense as a final, finishing layer on multilayered plywood, on finished planks, or, as is often the case, on finished articles such as furniture. This allows enough rare wood for everyone, since there would be very little available if it were used in planks.

The thin veneers are usually cut in a continuous strip by a special machine that slices off the soaked wood as the log is turned. The veneers are commonly $\frac{1}{32}$ inch or less in thickness (1 mm). They are also cut in the usual fashion, from one end of the log to the other, depending on the type of wood being used.

Plywood is composed of many layers of veneer, placed so that the grain of each layer is perpendicular to the preceding one. The layers are laminated together, yielding a sheet of wood which is stronger than the parts which make it up. There are many different types of plywood— rough on both sides, finished wood or fine wood veneer on one or both sides—and various thicknesses are available. Plywood may be used in articles where large sheets of wood are required or for objects where the edges will not be seen, since they are not as attractive as those made of standard wood.

As you begin to look for wood for your toys, you'll notice that the expressions softwood and hardwood come up frequently. These are classifications of wood, according to the type of tree from which the wood was obtained. Although they sound like descriptive terms, there are some softwoods that are actually harder than hardwoods and vice versa. Softwoods are woods that come from evergreen trees, which have the kind of leaves that are called needles. The conifers, or evergreens that bear cones, are thought to be the oldest type of trees on earth. Softwoods grow faster than hardwoods and are therefore less expensive. On the whole, they are softer and easier to use, especially when you are just starting out. White pine is probably the most widely available wood, readily found at lumberyards everywhere. It is so versatile and easy to work with that you may find it is the only wood you'll ever use.

Hardwoods come from trees with wide, flat leaves. These are called deciduous trees. Their wood is generally sturdier, slightly harder, and therefore harder to use at first, and somewhat more expensive. However, the dense, attractive grain and attractive tones produce a richer glow when finished and make them desirable for things you want to last.

Among the more readily found softwoods, aside from pine, the most prevalent are cedar, redwood, and Douglas fir. Cedar and redwood are good choices if you plan to make a wooden toy or other article that will be used outdoors. These woods have a natural resistance to mildew and dampness and actually become more interesting with age.

Popular hardwoods include oak, maple, cherry, walnut, and birch. In each case, the wood has a distinctive color and grain, and you'll enjoy looking at various samples once you've had a bit of experience and want to try a new look with a hardwood. Poplar, ash, chestnut, beech, sycamore, and cocobola are other hardwoods you may come across if you are looking in a well-supplied woodcraft supply house.

Exotic woods, as their name tells us, are the unusual woods, often reserved for fine furniture and marquetry—an inlaid wood veneer technique. These are the rare woods that are so often found in veneers. The most readily available exotic wood is mahogany, a hardwood that is within the realm of toy making as it is the least expensive of the exotics. Others, such as ebony and teak, are well known for their deep, rich hues. Rosewood, tulipwood, bird's eye maple, and zebrawood are among the rarest of woods, used almost exclusively in veneer form.

When you go to buy your first wood planks, you may find that several grades are offered. As there are several grading systems as well, it can be confusing. The grades, whichever names are given, refer to the quality of the board. On the whole, a premium grade is one that is relatively free from defects, such as knots and other weaknesses that can occur. This type of wood can be called clear, supreme, grade A, or better, all further grouped under the heading of select. Within the select grouping there are lesser grades, such as choice or grade B, then quality or grade C. These are all of better quality than the second general grouping, which is usually called common. These are boards often used in building and their quality is indicated by numbers, from one down to five, or names, the best being colonial, then sterling, utility, and industrial. To cloud the picture further, you'll find that these can be used only in reference to softwoods sold at lumberyards. For the most part, lumberyards don't carry the whole range of grades, so that your choice is made easier by the fact that it is limited by what's there.

As so much of the wood is visible in most toys, you'll find that you do want to use fairly good wood. Many lumberyards have one fine grade, one standard, and possibly one lesser grade. The finest in the case of pine is called clear pine. This means that almost all of the wood is free from defects. It also means that you're going to pay for the difference. If you can look at the wood before you buy, which you should, you may be able to find a bargain by looking at the common grade and finding a piece that has a lot of clear wood with an occassional blemish or knot.

You can then use this wood by not including the defects in your patterns as you mark the wood to cut it out. As so many toys have small parts that are put together, you'll be able to do this fairly often at quite a saving. To have a knot within a piece of the project—as long as it is a tight knot, which will not loosen and fall out—is not completely out of the question. And, if you like the look of painted toys, you can use a lesser grade of wood; the marks and defects can be filled in before painting.

In the case of hardwoods and the like, you'll discover that you will need to buy them from more specialized dealers. Woodworking stores and supply houses set up for woodcraft will usually carry only the best woods; all you need to do is select the type of wood that you want. However, do keep in mind that any wood that is widely available will generally be more expensive at a craft shop than at a lumberyard.

Whether you go to a lumberyard for the more standard types of wood or to a craft supply house for premium quality, hardwood, and unusual species, it's most important to know how much you want. Although you will always find a use for extra wood, you'll find that you get better service when you have a specific list of the required dimensions. If you note the width, thickness, and length of each board, you can concentrate on the selection of the kind or quality that you want. In some places there is a minimum charge per board. For example, if you want a few feet of a standard two by four, you may have to pay for a six-foot length. If this is the case—you should ask as the policy varies—then buy the entire length and save the rest for another project.

As wood is cut and planed, it becomes somewhat smaller; so the names of softwood planks refer to nominal sizes, not actual sizes. For example, a two by four is not really 2 inches by 4 inches, but something closer to $1\frac{5}{8}$ inches by $3\frac{5}{8}$ inches. This figure will vary from one plank to another. Since pine planks follow the general rule of being smaller than their names, the plans for all of the toys in this book are given with the true dimensions, called the finished sizes. For the names, use the following chart:

Thickness × Width	
Nominal Size (inches)	Actual Dimensions (inches)
¾ × 1	½ × ¾
¾ × 2	½ × 1⅝
¾ × 3	½ × 2⅝
¾ × 4	½ × 3⅝
1 × 1	¾ × ¾
1 × 2	¾ × 1⅝
1 × 3	¾ × 2⅝
1 × 4	¾ × 3⅝
1 × 6	¾ × 5½
1 × 8	¾ × 7¼
1 × 10	¾ × 9¼
1 × 12	¾ × 11¼
⁵⁄₄ × ⁵⁄₄	1 × 1
⁵⁄₄ × 2	1 × 1⅝
⁵⁄₄ × 3	1 × 2⅝
⁵⁄₄ × 4	1 × 3⅝
⁵⁄₄ × 6	1 × 5½
⁵⁄₄ × 8	1 × 7¼
2 × 2	1⅝ × 1⅝
2 × 4	1⅝ × 3⅝
2 × 6	1⅝ × 5½
2 × 8	1⅝ × 7¼
4 × 4	3⅝ × 3⅝

These are the most widely available sizes in standard lumber. There are also larger sizes, used in construction and such, that would not be suitable for toys, and smaller sizes, available in woodcraft supply houses, most often intended for the building of miniatures. Hardwoods are usually sold according to their actual dimensions. You can ask as you buy any wood to be sure. Whenever you can, you should buy in person to check on the quality of each board, and always feel free to question and possibly request a different one if you're not satisfied. Until your needs are known, you'll generally be better off if you select each one yourself. Bring a tape measure if you want to be sure of the actual dimensions of any board.

As you plan projects, you can keep the somewhat smaller dimensions of the boards in mind and work with them. You can assume that as the boards get wider, the difference between nominal size and actual size will increase. It's important to work with the nominal sizes as well as the true ones as you will order softwood by name, not finished size. When you have worked with wood for a while, this will not seem as odd as it does at first and you'll be able to use the names as you think of projects that are based on the corresponding actual dimensions.

The metric system of measurement is becoming more prevalent. If you find wood in metric sizes, you can use the following chart to convert the sizes:

Inches	Millimeters
1/16	1.5
1/8	3
3/16	4.5
1/4	6
5/16	8
3/8	9.5
7/16	11
1/2	12.5
5/8	16
3/4	19
7/8	22
1	25
1 1/4	31
1 1/2	38
1 3/4	44
2	50.5
2 1/4	57
2 1/2	65.5
2 3/4	70
3	76
4	101.5
5	127
6	152
7	178
8	203
9	228.5
10	254
11	279
12	304.5

These figures are rounded off to the nearest half mm. You'll find that many conversions round off still more, so that there is an even number of millimeters to correspond to a familiar inch size. As examples, 1″ is usually given as 25 mm, 2″ as 50 mm, 3″ as 75 mm, 4″ as 100 mm, and 12″ or 1′ as 300 mm. One meter is just over a yard, and when you are buying wood that has millimeters as a thickness and width indicator, its length will be given in meters:

Feet	Meters
1	.3
2	.6
3 (1 yard)	.9
4	1.2
5	1.5
6	1.8
7	2.1
8	2.4
9	2.7

Here again, the nearest familiar size is often referred to, so that the standard six-foot length would be called two meters.

As you buy wood, you should think about whether you want to cut the lengths you need yourself from a piece of standard-length wood, or whether you want to have the lumberyard cut the lengths for you. There is something to be said for each method, although the custom cutting will naturally be much more expensive than doing it yourself. On the whole, it's best to cut your own wood. A handsaw will do the job and you'll be in complete control of which parts of each board are used. In this way, you can use less than perfect lumber and place your cuts so that the defects are eliminated. Few, if any, yards will do this for you. Also, the expense is greatly added to by the fact that not only do you pay for the cutting, but an indiscriminate use of the planks mounts up. For example, if you need a four-foot length, the usual two feet left over will go on the lumberyard's scrap pile. The small amount of time you save doesn't justify the cost of having the wood cut for you. But in situations where you are working on a great number of toys—perhaps for a fund-raising event—and you find that you need quite a few lengths of wood, you would be better off having the wood cut rather than cutting it yourself with the basic set of hand tools recommended for these toys. The lumberyard will naturally have power saws and will save you a lot of hand sawing. Just be sure to check on the price beforehand.

As you look around a wood supply place of any type, keep an eye out for odd piles of wood. These are the remains of large cutting jobs that have been done for others. They may be out of sight in a workroom, so that you must ask for them. They're called scrap, but often there are many usable lengths, just right for toys. When you discover a yard that does have scrap piles, you will find a bargain in wood.

Another thing to check is the oddments of wood that have been fashioned into shapes, usually for furniture manufacturers. Some wood stores carry these and they can suggest all kinds of toy ideas. Knobs and buttons make terrific wheels, unusual small shapes may conjure up a chess set; all sorts of potential forms exist. All you need do is allow your mind to explore the possibilities. Once you have made several toys following plans and patterns, you'll get to know the feeling of the wood, and basic shapes will start to suggest original toy ideas that will be uniquely yours.

3
Basic Tools
and Equipment

If you are just beginning to make things with wood, you may be unaware of how much you can accomplish with simple hand tools. Almost any toy that you can think of can be made with the most basic equipment. Many of these tools and materials can be found in the average household, so that you may be surprised at how many things you already have on hand. Power tools and other extensive woodshop equipment are mainly used for speedier results or specialized tasks. They can be thought of as extras, not essentials.

The articles you'll definitely need are:

a coping saw, with several blades, to cut shapes

a handsaw, to cut lengths of wood

a hand drill, with assorted drill bits, to drill holes ¹⁄₁₆″–¼″, or 1 mm–6mm

a C-clamp or vise, to hold the wood as you saw it

a try square, a sort of L-shaped ruler that marks and tests right angles

sandpaper, coarse, medium, and fine, for light shaping and finishing

a supply of dowels, in various diameters

wood glue

a ruler and a retractable tape measure

a compass, pencils, and tracing, carbon, and drawing paper to make and mark patterns

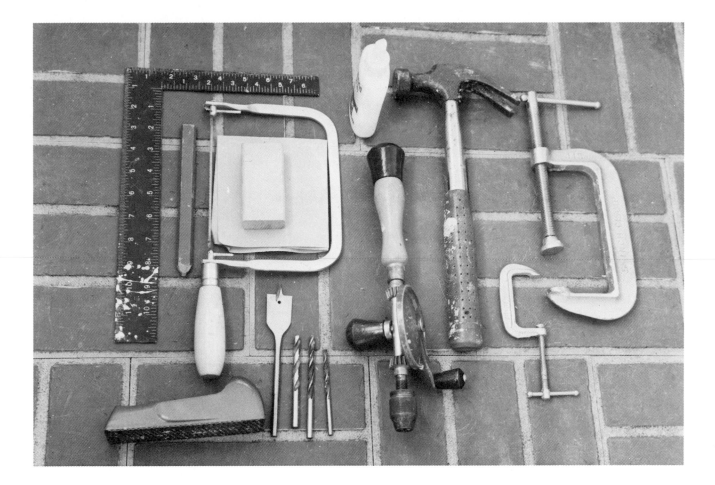

You'll also find it helpful to have:

a brace and assorted bits, to drill larger holes, from
 ½"–1¼", or 12 mm–31mm
a surform, to shape wood by filing
a plane, to finish wood by scraping
a pair of long-nosed pliers
an adjustable wrench
a level, which also checks angles
a hammer, finishing nails, and brads
screwdrivers, screws, nuts, and bolts of various sizes
an awl

These two basic groups of tools will allow you to perform all sorts of woodworking tasks. If you plan to buy
everything, you'll find that you can start out with the first
set. Then, you can add to your collection with the tools
you discover you need to do the type of work you enjoy
most. A possibility is to think of anyone you know who

has woodworking equipment you can use, perhaps in exchange for one of the toys you make with it. If not, all of these tools can be bought at reasonable cost and are well worth owning. It's best to buy fine quality tools as they work better and last longer. Keep the tools in a specific arrangement so that the next time you need a tool, it will be ready for you.

When you plan to do a fair amount of woodwork, a workbench with a built-in vise and lots of spaces to put all your equipment is a sound investment. Otherwise, you can use any sturdy table or other surface that you don't have to worry about. It's a good idea to set up a work area that is accessible and in a location where you won't have trouble cleaning up. If you have limited space, you can still work with ease as long as you maintain the tools in an organized manner, even in a specific drawer to keep them out of the way when you're not using them.

Tools are generally classified by the tasks that they perform. As you go to buy them, you'll discover that there are several types within each category.

Saws: There are many kinds of saws. Basically, they all cut wood, but each is intended for a certain job. As you cut across the grain, or up and down growing cells, it is called crosscutting. When you cut along the grain, it is called ripping. There are saws made for each purpose, the difference being the number, shape, and size of the teeth. A good basic handsaw, used to cut off lengths of wood (crosscutting) with eight or ten teeth per inch will be best. Ripsaws have fewer teeth, and crosscut saws can have up to thirty-two, but the types of cutting you are going to do can be accomplished with the one saw.

A coping saw is used for contour cutting, that is the cutting of shapes in wood. Its thin adjustable blade can cut at angles, around curves, and within wooden outlines to create the shapes needed for many toys. The blade is set into a sort of C-shaped holding frame which has a wooden handle. The best type to buy has a sturdy, rigid frame. The blades are attached to it by locking pins or other devices and they can be turned and held at an angle in the frame, letting you cut in any direction. Several extra blades are always worth having, and they come in different weights for finer or coarser cutting. You'll find that the blade needs to be replaced from time to time, even when you use the same weight, so it's helpful to buy a few at once.

Other saws, which are not specifically needed, may be used, if you have access to them, for special jobs. A backsaw, or tenon saw, is a short crosscut saw with a rectangular blade that has a strengthening metal spine along the top edge. It has fine teeth and cuts straight across the wood with a good degree of accuracy. Compass and keyhole saws have tapering narrow blades that fit into restricted areas for cutting out sections within a piece of wood; they can also be used for crosscutting small boards. A fretsaw is a variety of coping saw that has an elongated frame so that the saw can be used to cut within a larger sheet of wood than a standard coping saw. Its fine blades can make intricate shapes.

Drills and bits: To make holes in wood, for joining two parts with dowels, or to begin an inside cut so that you can slip in a coping saw blade to continue the cutting, you use a drill. The standard hand drill looks like an egg beater; the crank on the side is turned to rotate the bit, which is set into the bottom of the drill. An automatic drill is one that turns as you push it down from the top, but you won't really need one. The bits for a hand drill come in sizes from $\frac{1}{16}''-\frac{1}{4}''$ or 1 mm–6 mm and are used for most drilling operations. If you want to make larger holes, a brace is required. It is a kind of sideways U-shaped crank. At the top is a round handle, and the bits are fitted into the bottom. The bit turns as you hold the handle and rotate by holding the bottom of the U shape. The brace can hold bits which range in size from $\frac{3}{16}''-1\frac{1}{4}''$. The most usual bits are called auger bits, which have a starting spur that looks like a small screw and then the larger drilling diameter. Expansive bits, which make holes from $1''-2''$, or $2''-3''$, are available. Another special bit is called a Forstner bit. This has no spur and is used when you want to make a larger hole that will not go all the way through the wood.

Clamps and vises: As you cut wood with a handsaw or coping saw, you'll find that the job goes much more easily when the wood is held in one position and you have both hands free. In woodworking shops this is done by a vise, usually built into a table or workbench. You can buy a vise which will attach to any work surface, but you'll be surprised at their prices. A suitable alternative is a large C-clamp. You'll find these in a range of sizes. A 6″, which refers to the opening between the two holding parts of the clamp, is a good all-around size to buy. In metric sizes, this C-clamp is called a 15 mm. An extra clamp, of 4″–5″ will always come in handy.

Try squares and measuring devices: A try square or carpenter's square is an essential measuring and marking device. It is an L shape, often marked with inches along both sides of the L. Its basic purpose is to insure that you mark really straight lines at true right angles. In woodworking, it is also used to check that the wood is square in relation to itself; that is, that all of the corners are true right angles. Try squares come in a wide range of sizes and styles. Some are all metal, some are part metal and part wood, some have no measurement markings. Buy one that you like, preferably marked for easy reference. A good ruler, either made out of metal or with a metal edge set into wood, is also needed. If you can find one, a ruler marked with both inches and millimeters will be useful. The ruler is sometimes used as a straight edge and to help check squareness and alignment, so that a metal one is your best bet. To measure long pieces, buy a flexible metal or synthetic tape measure. Folding yardsticks, of various sizes up to 6′ are also handy for this purpose.

Sanding and shaping devices: Sandpaper is utilized in two general ways. The first, and most common, is for the smoothing and finishing of wood. A fair degree of shaping or changing the contours can also be effected with the coarser grades of sandpaper. You should buy a good assortment of weights, from the coarsest, which takes off a lot of wood and leaves a very rough surface, to the finest, used for smoothing and finishing. Sandpaper can be held on a comfortably sized block of wood, or you can buy a holder made for the job.

To shape wood more substantially, a surform or file is necessary. For making toys, most of this type of work can be done with patience and sandpaper, but you may want to buy a surform if a sculptural carved look appeals to you. It is an openwork metal filing piece set into a handle, and comes in various sizes. A small one will be fine for most things. As you work, the sawdust created by the filing action goes through the openings in the metal so that you don't have the problem of clogging that can occur with metal files.

Files come in many shapes with different surface filing configurations. The basic categories are the flat, round, and half round; these refer to the shape of a cross section of the file. The flat is used for straight surfaces and those which curve out, the half round for curves that go in, and the round for inside work where a flat file won't fit. The cut refers to the parallel lines which do the actual filing. These are placed on the surface of the file on a diagonal and can be single or crossing in a double-cut file. These lines are called teeth. They can also be curved, in a series of arcs, or (in a rasp) arranged in what looks like a series of raised triangles which file off a lot of wood with each stroke. These types are further characterized by their weight or coarseness, which ranges from "dead smooth" to rough. If you want to try out a file, there is a combination file which has four different types of filing surface and is suitable for general work. For these toys, however, several weights of sandpaper, and possibly a surform, are more than sufficient.

Planes are used for smoothing and shaping. They are adjustable and have a blade set inside which files off wood in shavings. They serve to even out a board that is not truly square and to make angled edgings on wood so that there are no sharp corners. A spokeshave is a similar device, with two small handles on either side of a blade for doing edgings. On the whole, you won't need either, as edges can be nicely finished with sandpaper.

Pliers and wrenches: There are many different kinds of pliers and wrenches, all of which are used for various holding duties. They are often needed to set a bolt, by holding the nut as it is screwed on. A pair of long-nosed pliers can be helpful in many situations. The most versatile type of wrench has an adjustable grip that is available in several sizes. The gripping surfaces of the wrench are adjusted by a turnscrew in one handle so that one medium-sized wrench can be used in place of a set of fixed-size wrenches. It's also quite handy to have one for many jobs around the house, especially for tightening bicycles and such.

Levels: A level is a device with small visible glass tubes set into a rectangular metal bar. The tubes are almost filled with greenish yellow alcohol. An air bubble is trapped in each tube, which is marked with two lines. These lines show the center of the tube, where the bubble will be when the level is parallel to the ground, or placed on work that is level. There can be one to three or more tubes. The main one checks levelness. The additional ones check perpendicularity and true ninety-degree angles. Levels are essential in building and making furniture, or anything else that depends on being level to be successful.

Hammers and nails: There is little hammering in toy making, as nails are less desirable than other means of assembling toys. Nails are the fastest means of attachment, but they can split the wood and the strength with which you hit them can damage it. If you're buying one, get a medium- to lightweight claw hammer, which can pull out nails with the claw. Flathead, common nails are sized according to an archaic system, the pennyweight, abbreviated by the English *d*, for penny. The smallest is a 2d, and they go up to a 60d, 6″ nail, with the sizes from 2d to 20d being most widely used. The following chart shows their sizes:

Nail Size	Head Diameter (inches) (divide by 3 for shank)	Length (inches)
2d	11/64	1
3d	13/64	1¼
4d	16/64 (¼)	1½
5d	16/64	1¾
6d	17/64	2
7d	17/64	2¼
8d	18/64	2½
9d	18/64	2¾
10d	10/32	3
12d	10/32	3¼
16d	11/32	3½
20d	12/32	4
30d	14/32	4½
40d	15/32	5
50d	16/32 (½)	5½
60d	17/32	6

Nails are sold by weight, usually per pound. As the size of the nail increases, the number per pound naturally decreases. To see just what the most used sizes look like, refer to the actual-size diagram of nails. As you can see, the flat heads of common nails are fairly large. You would not want them to be seen if you did use nails in any of your toys. For this reason, the type of nail known as a finishing nail is preferable. These are nails that have small heads, sometimes called brad heads, which can be driven, or set, below the surface of the wood where they are often covered by a dab of putty. The somewhat narrower shanks and sharp diamond-shaped tips make these nails less likely to mar the appearance of the finished joining. A small punchlike device is used with a hammer to drive these nails below the surface. It is called a nail set and usually comes in ½₂", ½₆", and ¼" sizes. The nails themselves are most often found in the following sizes:

Nail Size	Length (inches)	Usual Amount in a Pound
2d	1	1200
3d	1¼	800
4d	1½	550
5d	1¾	450
6d	2	300
7d	2¼	250
8d	2½	200
9d	2¾	150
10d	3	100
12d	3¼	80
16d	3½	75
20d	4	50

Brads are the same type of nails as finishing nails; they are just smaller. They range in size from ³⁄₁₆″ to 3″, in ⅛″ increments. Their shanks and heads remain smaller than a finishing nail of the same length. In all cases, you can buy fewer than one pound offers; you will do well with an assortment of the smaller sizes in finishing nails and brads.

Screwdrivers and screws, nuts and bolts: For a sturdy joining of two parts of wood, screws are often a better choice than nails. They form a nicer attachment, can be taken out easily, and when set in properly, with a drilled pilot hole to start the screw, they don't damage the wood or weaken it with the pounding of a hammer. Screwdrivers come in various lengths and sizes to fit various situations and screws. The names of the screwdrivers tell you their length. The width of the driving end or blade is chosen according to the size of the slot that runs across the top of each screw. For best results, the blade should match the size of the slot. That's why you need several different sizes.

There are several types of screws. The most widely used is the standard slotted flathead, or bright screw. There are

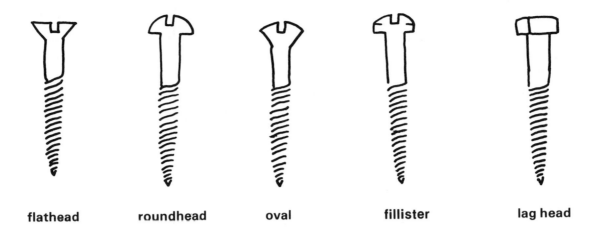

flathead **roundhead** **oval** **fillister** **lag head**

also round, oval, fillister and square- or lag-head screws, as shown in the comparative diagram. The lag screws are put in with a wrench, since, unlike the rest, they have no slots. They come in shiny, silver-colored, bright, galvanized, blued, or brass finishes. The brass ones don't rust, come in small sizes, and are particularly attractive. The standard sizes are:

Screw Size	Length (inches)
0	⅛
1	³⁄₁₆
2	¼
3	⅜
4	½
5	⅝
6	¾
7	⅞
8	1
9	1⅛
10	1¼
11	1⅜
12	1½
14	1¾
16	2
18	2½
20	3
24	3½

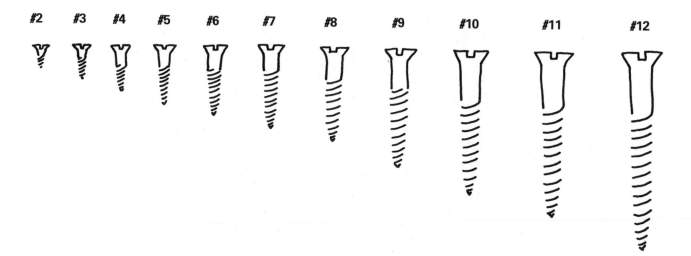

The most widely used sizes, shown in the actual-size diagram are the 2 through 12.

Phillips head screws have an X-shaped opening, which requires a Phillips head screwdriver. They slip less as they are screwed in and can be easier to use for this reason. They come in a similar range of sizes.

Bolts, secured by nuts at their threaded bottoms, are stronger than screws or nails. Bolts are set into holes drilled all the way through the wood parts. The nut is often held away from the wood by a washer, or small metal ring, that is slipped onto the shank of the bolt before the nut is screwed on. Bolts come in a number of different sizes, styles, and lengths. The flathead stove bolt, which looks like a standard screw, and round head stove bolt are most often used. Carriage bolts have a smooth round top and are difficult to remove once they are in place. For bolt setting, you'll need an adjustable wrench, or set of wrenches, and a suitably sized screwdriver.

Awls: An awl looks like a short ice pick. It is used for marking holes by making a depression with its sharp point, for making small holes, and for scribing or marking wood by scratching its surface.

Compass, pencils, and tracing, carbon, and drawing paper: One of the most important parts of woodworking is making accurate patterns and marking them precisely on the wood. Compasses are used to make curves, circles, and to help mark off the exact centers of areas. They can also help in marking equal spaces. The various types of paper are used to copy and enlarge patterns, and then to transfer them onto the wood. If you want to create your own toy designs, you may find it easier to work with graph paper, as the marked squares insure an accurate rendition of your idea.

Wood glue and wooden dowels: The most attractive, natural way to assemble the parts of wooden toys is with wood glue and, where needed, wooden dowels in short lengths. This type of assembly requires a bit more time and preparation but in the long run it is by far the best. There are many different kinds of glue which you can use. Modern glues are almost all made from synthetics, and there are quite a few that are solely made for joining wood. Any one of these will be good to use. Even plain white liquid glue is a possibility. A pale tan glue, that comes in the same type of squeeze bottle as the white glue, is particularly handy and is quite strong. It alone, without doweling or other supports, is often sufficient to join the parts of many toys. Epoxies are sometimes recommended, but they are mixed using equal parts from two tubes and can be quite messy.

Wooden dowels are made out of hardwood. They are long sturdy rods. They come in several lengths, the most usual being 18″ and 3′, and many diameters from ⅛″ to 3″. They are invaluable in toy making; you should get a good supply and always have some on hand. The most versatile sizes are the smaller ones, especially with a crank type hand drill. The dowels are fitted into spaces made by the drill bits, so that you use the sizes that correspond.

Other tools: When you go to a hardware store to buy your tools, you'll be confronted by an incredible number of tools and accessories. Many of these are variations or refinements of basic tools. Others are used for tasks which are relatively rare in toy making. Still others can make your projects go a little more smoothly and might find a place in your workshop once you have done a few toys and plan to make many more. For example, an accessory tool like a miter box, which is used with a crosscut or backsaw as a guide while sawing straight across or on an angle, is very useful if you do a lot of hand sawing. To cut the lengths you need from a longer plank, a simple wood miter box can be a good investment. But, you may find that you cut well without it, or that you are going to order precut pieces, or that you'll use a friend's power saw. None of these things can really be predicted. You have to get used to your own pace and methods of working before you can really know which extras will be the ones you want. There is great latitude in what each woodworker considers to be essential. The only way to discover your own set of essentials is to develop your skills with hand tools and see where your interests lead.

Power tools: For almost every hand tool, there is a power tool counterpart. Power tools don't necessarily do the job better, but they certainly do it faster. Many people who have been working with wood for years swear by their hand tools and wouldn't give them up for any power tools. Others prefer to do some things with hand tools and some with power tools. It's a matter of personal preference.

There is a wide range of stationary power tools, all of which share the feature of being very expensive. There are band and scroll saws for shaped cutting, circular and chain saws for crosscutting and ripping, drill presses which drill precise holes, orbital sanders, lathes for turned work; the list could go on and on. These are intended for professional workshops. There are versions of these tools on a smaller scale for home workshops for those who wish to make a substantial investment in equipment.

A suitable alternative for those who want the speed of power tools is the growing number of portable models. Of these, the ones that would have the greatest appeal to toymakers are the saber saw and the drill. A portable saber saw has a fairly short blade that cuts by moving up and down. You hold the saw somewhat like an iron and the blade is at the bottom. There are many blades available for different cutting needs. You can use a saber saw for ripping, crosscutting, and contour cutting. A good accessory for it is a small table in which you place the saw upsidedown, with the blade sticking up through the table. This allows you to have both hands free to guide the wood as you cut.

Portable power drills drill holes and can be fitted with discs for sanding. There is a large number of bits you can buy that make holes ranging from the tiniest $\frac{1}{64}$" up to $1\frac{1}{2}$". There is also an expansive bit for holes up to 2" and another for holes up to 3", and screwdriver bits. For the almost effortless drilling of holes, try a power drill, available in a variety of sizes and models.

If you have access to power equipment, you should try it out, preferably with someone who knows how to use it safely. Another way you can test power tools that you think you may want to buy is to rent a portable model from a hardware store or lumberyard. The only one you might want is the saber saw, mainly for cutting lengths of wood, as a handheld coping saw can be more accurate for contour cutting. Before you buy one, rent the same model and give it a good workout. You may discover that you don't really need it and it's a lot easier to return the rented one.

Safety: When you start to work with wood, it is very important to develop safe working habits. If you treat all of your tools with the proper respect, they'll give you years of faithful service. Find a definite location for each article and put it there as soon as you finish with it. Never leave anything lying around, where it could be knocked off a table or accidentally get caught up in the work you are doing.

Get a plastic box with lots of compartments for all of your small fittings and accessories. When you start to use a tool, check it out. Make sure that all handles are secure and tight and blades and bits are sharp. Since you will, for the most part, be working with softwood, remember that tools get dull fairly fast when working with it. Dull tools are less efficient and more likely to cause problems. Have crosscut saws sharpened by a professional and replace coping sawblades often. Wear protective goggles, safety shields, or glasses. Work gloves are also good. If you find them too cumbersome, wear an old pair of thin leather gloves. As you work, remember to keep your hands out of the way as much as possible. If you have long hair, tie it back. At first, these preparations will seem bothersome, but after a while they'll be second nature and you'll be much happier when you do it right. Most of all, keep all tools and materials out of the reach of children. Children are fascinated by tools and will try them out if they find them. A good solution to this is to make, or buy, a child's workbench with harmless toy tools, and keep yours where they cannot be obtained.

4
Woodworking Procedures

To make toys of wood, there are a number of standard procedures for setting up a pattern to follow, cutting it out, and assembling the parts into a toy. As you follow plans for any project in wood, you'll discover that it is assumed that you know how to do the various things needed to make it up. There is no explanation of technique, just the dimensions and what to do, not how to do it. For those who have never made anything in wood, the very appearance of a plan may seem mysterious. And yet, these steps are simple to master and patterns are quite easy to understand, once you know how. You'll be pleased at how quickly you'll be ready to make your first toy. As you learn the techniques, it's always a good idea to try them out on some scrap lumber. If you practice a little, quite soon you'll gain a lot of experience and the understanding that comes with it.

Working plans: A woodworking plan shows you all of the component parts needed to create an article. The drawings in a plan are intended to show you how the construction is achieved. To do this in the least space, a sort of visual shorthand is used. Most commonly this takes the form of an exploded view, as it is called. In this type of presentation, each part of the object is shown in space, pulled away from its opposing part, but remaining in the same relationship in terms of assembly. In this manner, you know that if three parts are shown, for example, as being in a vertical stack, with one on the bottom, one in the middle, and one on top, with spaces between, it means that in the finished article they are fitted together in that order. The components are shown in this way so that information on dimensions and actual sequence of assembly is depicted without words. The scale, or relative size of each component is also given. Unless specified otherwise, all of the parts in any given plan are drawn to the same scale. This means that they are right in relation to each other; whether you make them larger, smaller, or leave them the same size, they will work together correctly.

Exploded views are most often shown in perspective. Other presentations are flat, in what is called a scale or elevation drawing. In this type of rendition, there are often three necessary views of each part for you to know what it will look like. The top, front, and side views are needed. In a perspective drawing, the view from the front is given, with the sides and top shown as part of the one drawing. For basic constructions, an exploded view is often unnecessary. As the parts are easy to put together, the important thing is showing their precise dimensions.

Some of the drawings in this book are smaller than actual size. In most cases, the actual dimensions are given on each part, and you can work with these. In projects where the shapes are unusual, the outside dimensions of each shape are given so that you can make your own grid and trace and enlarge the pattern to full size according to the instructions below.

Another means of presenting parts, used quite a lot for oddly shaped pieces, is to show the part on a grid of lines drawn into squares. These squares allow you to enlarge the pattern successfully. They are used in two ways. The first, commonest method, is to present the shape within a series of squares that are smaller than, but represent, one inch. You simply take a sheet of drawing paper and mark out the same number of squares of one inch each. Then you copy the drawing into the squares, one by one. Even if you don't think that you can draw, this somehow works every time. Another way in which squares are used is for an indeterminate sized object, which can be enlarged as much, or as little, as you like.

Another marking that you are likely to see on plans is an arrow within each shape. This is used in cases where the grain, or direction of the wood fibers, is important to the outcome of the piece. For example, an arrow pointing to the side means that you place the pattern part on the wood so that the grain is running along in the same direction as is the arrow. If the arrow points up or down, you place the part so that the grain goes that way.

Along with the dimensions of all the parts, the order of assembly, and the direction of the grain, plans tell you how much wood you will need, and in which sizes, to complete the project. In most presentations, the finished size of the lumber is given, not the nominal size. This is to avoid the confusion that might ensue if the names were used. Any fittings, such as dowels, screws, or whatever, are listed. In this way, you can have everything ready as you start to make the article.

For each of the toys, the information you need to make it is given in the form that best suits the particular toy. Many projects don't need exploded views because the parts are simple to put together once you have them cut out. But whenever there might be a question of how the parts fit, an exploded view, or completed diagram, will show you the answer.

Enlarging with squares: Grids are a very good way to enlarge pattern parts, even for articles which are drawn to scale. Although there are no squares given, you can make your own set to enlarge the diagram to the size you want. All you need is a few sheets of tracing paper, a few sheets of drawing paper, pencils, a ruler, and a try square or L-shaped ruler. To begin, take a sheet of tracing paper and place it on the diagram you want to enlarge. Trace the outlines exactly. Remove the paper and put it on a white sheet of paper on a work surface. The sheet underneath is there to make the tracing easier to see. Take the ruler and put it just under the bottom of the form. Draw a line that

has a complete inch measurement (no fractions) even if it extends a bit beyond the sides of the form. Then take the square or L-shaped ruler to form the sides and draw a rectangle or square around the shape, whichever fits best. Make sure that the sides have a complete inch measurement as well. In the example shown, the elephant is about 3¼″ by 4¼″, so the box around it is 4″ by 5″. It's easier to work with a full inch, and you can make the outline larger than is strictly necessary to reach an inch mark.

Then, using the ruler, mark off each inch within the outline. First do it just within the top and bottom lines, making a small dot at each inch. Then, using your dots as a guide, make lines across the interior of the outline. Do the same at the sides. You will now have a grid of one-inch square boxes. Next, take another sheet of drawing paper. To double the size in the example, you draw a rectangle that is 8″ × 10″. To double the size of any shape, you double the number of inches of the original outlines. Draw a grid of intersecting lines on the large outline, using 2″

per square. To transfer the shape onto the larger grid, make a small dot at each point on the large version where a pattern line on the small version crosses a line of the grid. The dots give you reference points to draw the shape. As you draw, square by square, you'll see the larger shape emerging. For a clean copy, cover the completed drawing with a sheet of tracing paper and trace the enlarged shape. For more intricate shapes, you can use smaller squares for the grids, such as ½″ markings on the original and 1″ on the larger one.

You can use this method to enlarge all sorts of shapes and forms. As it depends on the number of squares in the grid and not their dimensions, you can enlarge as much as you want, or change proportions. All you need to do is draw the outline and grid on a tracing of the small version. Then draw an outline in any larger size and mark off the same number of squares for the large grid. To change proportions somewhat, elongate the rectangle, or turn the square into a rectangle, in the large outline. Then mark off an equal number of boxes. This grid will be a series of rectangles, but as long as there are the same number, it will work.

The method is also used in reverse, when you want to make something smaller, going from the larger outline to a small one.

For diagrams that are marked with squares, usually the squares are one-inch scale, that is, they are not an inch but they stand for one. To enlarge one of these, merely draw a grid with the same number of squares, one inch each. You can also buy special paper, usually found in art supply stores, that is printed with one-inch squares. In this type of graph paper there are sometimes smaller squares within each one-inch area, but the one-inch squares have darker outlines. It is much easier to use as the squares are there. All you need to do is mark your outlines for the number of squares you need.

If you are still not convinced that you can draw an object, although the squares method simplifies the process, you can have a photostat made. In a photographic store, you can order photostats in any size that you want. They can be larger or smaller. They can't change proportions.

Making the pattern: When you have all of the parts you need in the right size, you have all of the pattern parts. You can use them as is, and transfer directly to wood using carbon paper and an empty ball-point pen. You place the carbon paper facedown on the wood and place the pattern on top. As you go over the outlines with the empty pen, they are marked on the wood by the carbon paper. If you're using a dark wood, you can buy pale carbon paper in art supply stores.

Another method of transfer is to glue the traced shapes onto cardboard with rubber cement and cut them out. The cutout parts are called templates and you use them to mark around with a soft pencil. To do this, you make the pattern beforehand. The templates can be glued to cardboard or transferred on with carbon paper and then cut out. Mark each one with grain lines, if needed, and how many of each should be cut. Any other information on the plan, such as placement of holes and the like, should be drawn on the template for handy reference. One benefit is that the pattern parts are now in a form that allows you to hold them together to see how they fit in the object itself.

Making original patterns: As you get used to working with plans for wooden articles, you'll be able to use paper patterns and templates to test out your own ideas. Once you have made up some templates and resulting toys following written plans, you'll find that variations will occur to you. Whatever you think of should be drawn on paper to see how it looks. Then you can make cardboard parts for the drawings that are most appealing. The parts can be assembled, in a mock-up of the actual toy, using tape. When you constantly experiment, you'll be happy to find that many of your concepts work well. The cardboard model can be untaped and used as the pattern for your toy.

For design ideas that come to you when you don't have the time to draw out and create an entire paper model, you can keep a notebook. When you think of a design, sketch it out and write down any notes or comments. A notebook of design ideas of this nature will become an invaluable woodworking tool. When you sketch out thoughts on toys that you want to make, even if you don't use them for a while, having a record will preserve them until you're ready. The best idea may slip away if you don't get it down on paper. As your collection of design possibilities grows, you'll have a great source of inspiration for your toy projects.

Marking the wood for cutting: The first step in marking the wood for cutting is to check each plank. Sometimes boards are not cut off at an exact right angle to the sides, often the end is cracked or split. Take the try square and test the end of the board by placing the short end of the square along a side, which you can usually assume will be straight. Look at the end of the board, just below the long end of the square. If it doesn't meet the square neatly all along the end, it means that it is uneven. Move the square down onto the board, with the short end going along the side. Take a pencil and mark a line across the board, on a true right angle to the side. If there are any splits, make the line below them as far into the board as needed to eliminate them completely from the good wood. Splits continue to crack apart if you don't cut them off.

This line is your reference point, sometimes called a datum line, used to set up the pattern as you plan the best use of the wood. If you have several pattern parts, put them on the wood and arrange them so that any knots or other defects are outside of their outlines whenever possible. You want to use only the clear wood for best results. When there are several different thicknesses of wood in a toy, be sure that you are placing each part on the correct thickness of wood. For large sheets, such as plywood, you may shift the parts around as needed to find the layout that best suits the wood, making the most with the least waste. If there are grain lines, follow them for the visible outer layer of plywood. Although the grain is less important as there are several layers laminated together and their grain runs in the opposite direction on every other layer, the grain direction is sometimes a visual part of the design. When you follow the visible layer for the grain, the piece will look as it was meant to.

Transfer all of the pattern pieces onto the wood. Use

either carbon paper and an empty pen, or templates and a soft pencil. It is sometimes recomended that an awl be used to scribe in the lines, but it can easily cut too deep.

When marking a pattern on pine and other softwoods, you can place the drawing on the wood and go over it with a pencil. The softwood is easily marked and the pencil lines show when you look at them closely. You can go over the outlines after the drawing has been removed, using the pencil to darken the marked lines. This eliminates the need for carbon paper. For hardwoods this won't work, as they don't pick up the impression made by a pencil.

To measure and mark out lengths of wood for pattern pieces that are merely cut into squares or rectangles, allow a little extra, about ⅛". This is for the width of the saw blade. When you merely mark the parts after measuring exactly, the center pieces will be a fraction too short. The best way to do these is to mark and cut one at a time, or if you prefer to do all the marking at once, leave a space of ⅛" between lines. If it has ruler markings, the try square and a soft pencil can be used to mark off the lines.

When you are marking a pattern that is essentially one large piece and you have a plank that is longer than you need, place the pattern on the wood before you cut off the length you want. When the length is cut first, you may find that you have included a knot and there isn't enough room left on the wood to move the pattern over and avoid the defect.

Once all of the pattern parts are marked, check to be sure that you have every one that you need. When you have a few parts on one plank, it's best to cut off each section as a block. It is then easier to cut out the shape itself. Make sure that there is enough room for cutting between each of the parts and that all straight cuts are marked on a true right angle to the long side of the plank. When you're sure the pattern is marked correctly, you're ready to cut it out.

Straight cutting: One of the basic procedures in woodworking is cutting straight across a board or crosscutting. To learn how to make a clean, straight cut is not as hard as you might think when you haven't done it before. Use a scrap piece of wood to practice or cut within the waste sections that you marked off on a pattern plank. On an extra plank, mark off a sample cut near the end of the board using a try square and soft pencil. Clamp the wood to your worktable, placing a small piece of wood between the clamp and the wood itself to protect it. This isn't strictly necessary on a practice piece, but it's a good habit to get into. The wood should extend beyond the clamp and off the edge of your worktable so that there are about three inches between the marked cutting line and the edge of the table.

If you're right-handed, stand on the left side of the plank and place your left hand on it, just behind the clamp. Reverse positions if you're left-handed. When using a vise, clamp the wood into it about 3″ from the cutting line. It is in the right position for cutting and you don't need to hold the plank at all. Hold the crosscut saw in your free hand loosely, with your index finger extended along the handle pointing toward the blade. Make sure that the saw blade is placed on the wood so that it is perpendicular to it. Put it on the thickness of the wood just a fraction of an inch away from the marked line. This allows for the width of the saw blade and its resulting cut, so that it is placed on the waste side of the line. When the wood is held in a C-clamp, you saw with the blade pointing down and saw toward you. In a vise, you saw with the blade pointing straight ahead, and saw down through the plank. Always saw through the thickness of the wood, not the width. Contrary to popular belief, the teeth of the saw work best when they cut as narrow a section as possible. There is less drag on the saw. When you angle it onto the face or width of the wood, it increases the size of the surface you are cutting and actually slows you down. A sharp saw will do the work for you. There's no need to exert a lot of pressure. Use your body to create a steady forward and back motion as you saw. Draw the saw up and back, with a steady, slow pace. It only cuts on the motion away from you, the drive motion, due to the angle of the teeth. There's a rhythm to sawing that develops quickly once you use the right technique.

Continue to saw until you get to the final part of the

cut. Then, support the end of the board, changing position if necessary so that it doesn't crack off before you can saw it off. That's all there is to it. Make several trial cuts, marking each with a square to practice cutting well-squared pieces. Remember to hold the saw more loosely than you might expect and to keep it perpendicular to the board, and you'll cut straight every time.

To cut off the sections for a pattern, you follow the same steps. Place the saw a fraction of an inch away from the line into the excess wood. For center cuts, saw in the ⅛" space you provided for this purpose. Cut off all of the lengths.

When you are working with plywood, you'll find it much easier to cut out the pattern shapes if you mark and cut the whole section out of the larger sheet. Prop the marked sheet of plywood against the worktable so that the section extends beyond the side of the table. Clamp it in place, clamping to a leg of the table, so that the plywood is held upright. Then, saw through the thickness to cut out the pattern section. Change the position of the plywood to make the second cut, completely cutting out the area in which the pattern pieces fall. For very large parts, this step can be eliminated as they are just as simple to cut themselves.

Contour cutting: Cutting out shapes with a coping saw in the step known as contour cutting is enjoyable, once you get the hang of it. The saw has an adjustable blade whose angle can be set in the handle for cuts that move in different directions. The metal frame holds the blade taut for cutting. As you look at the saw, you'll see how the blade is set into the holding pieces at the top and bottom of the frame. Usually the blade has a tiny bar through the top and one through the bottom. These bars fit into the metal fittings on the frame by merely sliding in place. The coping saw comes with a blade in place, but you should open it up to see how it works. Grasp the handle with one hand and the rod extending out from the bottom fitting with the other hand. Turn the handle counterclockwise to loosen the blade. The bottom fitting also holds the handle on; it ends in a large screw, like a threaded shank. As you unscrew it, the frame opens out a bit. The blade comes out of the fittings, and if you keep unscrewing, the handle will come off. It's not necessary to take off the handle when you change blades, just loosen it as needed. Replace the blade and rescrew the handle until the blade is taut. You'll notice that the blade can be put in so that the teeth point down toward the handle or up toward the top fitting. This is really a matter of personal preference. When the blade points down, the cut is made on a pull stroke (as you bring the saw toward you) if the saw is held horizontally, or on a down stroke if the saw is held vertically. When the teeth point up, the blade cuts on the drive stroke (as you push it away from you) if the saw is horizontal, or on an up stroke if it is vertical. You can try both positions to see which you like better. Whichever you choose, always make sure that the rods which extend out from the top and bottom fittings are in the exact same position in relation to one another. They move in order to change the angle on the blade, and if they aren't the same, the blade is twisted and it will snap when you try to cut with it. For your first trial cuts, place the blade so that the angle is straight and they face directly out.

A sort of holding block, made by cutting a large V shape in the end of a plank, as shown, can be quite useful for

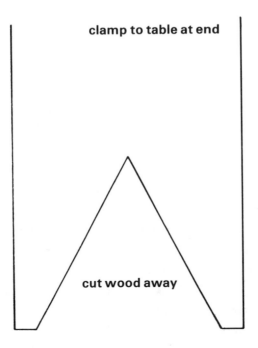

clamp to table at end

cut wood away

cutting with a coping saw. The plank is clamped to your work table and the part to be cut is placed between the tips of the V, in the space. You then hold the wood with your free hand. For a steadier cut, use another clamp to hold the wood on the plank. You can also work with a vise by merely clamping the wood into it. For practice, you can cut an unmarked piece of wood to see how the saw works. Then, draw on basic curves, and gradually increase the number of bends and angles, so that you learn how to cut in all directions.

The coping-saw blade is thinner than a crosscut saw, so that you don't have to cut too far off the line. Hold the saw perpendicular to the wood and saw with a steady up and down motion. Make the maximum use of each stroke, cutting with the entire length of the blade, not just the center. For thicknesses of up to ½", you can saw at a steady rate. For thicker woods, you should pause occasionally because the friction of sawing heats up the tin blade and it may break unless it has a chance to cool off.

To cut a curve, you move the wood in relation to the saw, always maintaining a ninety-degree angle on the saw blade. When you keep the saw in a straight up and down position, you make a neat cut that is square and even.

To cut more intricate shapes, you change the position of the blade in its holder. At the outer top, above the top fitting, there are marked angle lines you can use as a guide to shift the position of the blade. Here again, the top and bottom rods should be in the same position relative to one another to insure that the blade isn't twisted.

As you cut, you'll see how the saw works. It can only be used to cut into wood as far as its holder allows. That's one of the only limitations on the variety of shapes you can cut with a coping saw. When you work on pieces that are no more than 10" wide or long, you'll be able to cut right in to the center if you want, as the opening in the saw is 5". This is also the reason why you'll find it best to cut off lengths of wood for a pattern part before you shape with a coping saw.

You may notice that the bottom of the cut wood is not as neatly cut off as the top. This sometimes happens, and to prevent it when cutting actual project parts, get a few pieces of inexpensive thin wood, such as ⅛″ plywood and use one under the actual wood as you cut it out. The thin wood will take the uneven cutting at the bottom and your parts will be perfect.

A variation of this technique is to sit down and cut with the saw held horizontally. If you have a vise, this is a good method to use as the wood is held vertically in a vise. Otherwise, you may find it too difficult to support the wood to try this technique.

Using a fretsaw: A fretsaw is very similar to a coping saw, but it has a much wider opening between the blade and the back of the frame. This allows you to cut into wood of greater proportions, up to 20″ wide or long. The fine blade is not adjustable in angle, but it is thin enough to go around the shapes you need without needing to be turned in the handle as a coping-saw blade is. The blade is set so that the teeth point toward the handle and it cuts on the down stroke. Be sure that you go slowly and pause now and then. The fine blade is more likely to snap from overheating than a coping-saw blade, so that you have to watch it.

Incised cutting: Cutting shaped within a piece of wood, completely surrounded by wood without a cut in it, is called incised or enclosed cutting. It creates a nice effect and is easy to do with a coping saw as long as the wood is not too large. For larger pieces of wood, the same steps are followed, using a fretsaw. The compass saw or keyhole saw is often recommended for this, and they will work for incised cuts that are very basic in shape, but their blades are too big to make intricate turns.

To make an enclosed cut, you begin by marking the shape. For practice, make a fairly simple shape within a piece of scrap wood. Drill a hole, as described later in this chapter, at one of the corners or points in the shape. The hole should be on the inside or waste section of the incised cut. Open the blade in your coping saw or fretsaw and slip it into the hole. Close the handle around the blade and saw as usual. With a coping saw, adjust the angle of the blade as needed to change directions. For a fretsaw, turn the wood as needed.

Cutting with a saber saw: A portable power saber saw can save a great deal of time in cutting. If you buy or rent one, be sure to get the instructions that come with the saw. Read them a couple of times until you know all of them well. This is an important step and should not be skipped. There are many different blades, for all sorts of cutting jobs, and attachments to make straight and circular cuts. The attachments aren't really needed if you work carefully.

Fit an appropriate blade into the saw, according to its directions in the accompanying instructions. Mark cutting lines on a practice piece. The wood is held flat, between two tables or other surfaces. You cut by turning on the saw and bringing it to the edge of the wood. It cuts quickly, so that you should get a bit of practice in guiding it correctly. Make sure that everything but the wood to be cut is completely out of the way, especially your free hand. At first, you can use two hands to guide the saw to be sure. You follow the marked cutting lines, moving the saw across them.

Once you get used to the sound and vibration of a saber saw, it is easy to use. You can cut lengths of wood and large shapes. For more intricate shapes and outlines, a coping saw will work better than a saber saw.

Drilling holes: Drilling holes is simple to do. The tricky part is getting them to go straight through the wood on a true perpendicular. Take one of the pieces of wood that you've cut off in learning the sawing technique and clamp it onto the table so that the end extends beyond it. Make several marks with an awl, both to mark the holes and to start them. Choose any drill bit and fit it into the chuck, or holding ring, at the bottom of your hand drill. The surrounding ring screws closed and tightens around the bit to hold it in the drill.

Hold the top knob in one hand and the rotating wheel in the other and place the drill on one of the marks. Be sure that it is straight up and down. To test it, place your try square alongside and use it as a guide until you're used to the feeling of the correct holding position. Keep the drill in that position and rotate the wheel at a steady pace. You push down from the top to start the hole. There's no need to really press on it, as the bit cuts into the wood almost on its own once it has been started.

Make a number of holes, testing with the square until they come out straight without it. To use a brace and bits, you follow the same procedure. The only difference is the way in which you turn the brace to do the drilling. You hold the top knob with one hand and grasp the outermost side of the brace with the other. Then, use the square to be sure that the brace is perpendicular and rotate the side in a complete circle as you drill. The brace moves around under the top knob, which is held absolutely steady.

Sometimes the wood tends to splinter a bit when the drill bit breaks through to the other side. To prevent this when drilling holes for a project, clamp an extra piece of wood underneath the one being drilled. For smoother drilling, take a piece of paraffin or a plain white candle and rub it up and down along the bit before you start to drill.

To drill holes that go only partway through the wood you need to use a guide. There are special bit gauges sold for this, and they adjust to show you when to stop. They work well as long as you stop immediately. Otherwise they scratch the wood around the hole.

There are two other ways that you can prepare the drill bit for part-way holes. The first is to take a piece of cloth tape or masking tape and tape it around the bit, with the desired length of the bit remaining below the tape. As you drill, the tape goes toward the wood. When you reach the tape you know that the hole is the right depth and you stop drilling. Another method is to take a block of wood, $1'' \times 1''$ and as long as required, slip it on the drill bit and leave the lower portion, the desired depth of the hole, exposed. Then you drill a hole, $\frac{1}{4}''$ larger than the bit you are going to use, straight through the block. The block is then placed on the drill bit to drill the part-way hole. Once you reach the right depth, the drilling is automatically stopped as the block prevents the bit from going any farther. This method takes more preparation but is very accurate, and you'll find that you use the block on many occasions.

To drill partway into wood with a brace, make sure that you use a plain bit, or a Forstner bit. With an auger bit the screwlike spur will mar the inside of the hole and make it deeper than you planned. It can also break through to the other side of the wood if there is only a small amount left below the hole.

Drilling holes with a portable power drill: For fast, efficient hole drilling, you can use a portable power drill. There are many varieties, which take different ranges of bit sizes. The most basic one will drill a good assortment of sizes up to 1½″ in diameter. Read the instruction booklet that comes with the drill to get to know all of its workings. There is a small keylike device, used to open and expand the chuck which holds the bits. Tape the key to the wire with electric tape, and you'll always know where it is. When loose, they have a tendency to disappear when you need them most.

All portable power drills not only drill holes but can also be used with sanding discs and screwdriver bits. Some can go in reverse, hold very large auger bits and the like, or have variable speeds. All the operations of the one you are using are detailed in the instructions for the specific model.

To drill holes, you place the desired size bit into the chuck, opening it and then closing it with the key. You can hold the wood in either a vertical position and aim the drill horizontally, or in a horizontal position and aim the drill straight down. Usually, the first method is used when you have a vise to hold the wood. Make as many practice holes as you like to see the position you need for truly straight holes.

Sanding: When making a toy, the first sanding is done after you cut out the parts and drill all holes, *before* you put it together in any way. If you assemble the toy first, you'll find that many areas of it are hard to reach, resulting in an uneven surface. The extent of the sanding depends on the surface of the wood and the kind of finish you want it to have. At this point, the sanding is done to smooth the wood, take off any remaining marks that the pencil or carbon paper have left, and to reach all areas, including those which will be placed together in assembly.

Take a sheet of medium sandpaper and run its smooth side on the edge of your worktable. This softens up the paper a little, making it easier to use. Cut it into quarters and wrap one around a small wood block, or place it in a sandpaper holder. Run the sandpaper along the wood, always following the grain. If you go against the grain, it will make scratches in the wood which are surprisingly hard to remove. Sand lightly, and change to a finer grade of paper as soon as all of the areas have been done. You merely want to smooth the wood; it will be finished later on, so don't sand off the corners where the wood has been cut. To reach into curves, wrap one piece of paper around a thick dowel.

When you plan to make a highly polished surface, you should sand again with the finest paper, or garnet paper. The final finish depends on how smooth the wood is, and any finish you put on a badly sanded piece will only emphasize the surface, not cover it.

When all of the areas have been sanded with fine paper, you are ready to assemble the toy. As the sanded wood is very clean and smooth, you'll want to keep it that way as you assemble it.

Bonding parts together: Bonding, or gluing, wood parts together is an effective way to assemble many joinings in toymaking. When you use wood glue, following the right procedure, you get a good, sturdy attachment. You can use any glue that is made for the purpose. Keep it at room temperature and tightly covered so that it doesn't get thick. As you use glue, don't let it get on any of the visible parts of the wood; it's hard to take off without damaging the surface. You'll also need a clamp or two of the right size to hold the parts together as they dry. To protect the wood, special clamps called veneering clamps may be used, or you can put two thin scraps of wood or thick cardboard between the wood and a standard C-clamp.

Check the parts to be glued to make sure that they are

perfectly clean. Place them together to see where to put the glue and whether they meet completely. Gaps in meeting can't be filled with glue; they are sanded to fit if necessary. When you have cut the parts carefully, this is rarely needed. Spread a thin layer of glue on each side of the parts to be joined. Place them together carefully. Clamp the two parts together. If any excess glue runs out, wipe it off right away. Leave the wood clamped together for at least twenty-four hours, so that you're sure it's dry. When it is very humid, wait for two days.

Laminating is the bonding of two or more layers of wood. It is done extensively in veneering and in toy making to make a thicker piece or section than you would be able to cut out with a coping saw. If, for example, you want a solid block that is 3″ thick, you can cut two 1½″, or three 1″ pieces. Then, you spread a thin layer of glue on each of the sides to be joined and clamp them all tightly together until they are completely dry.

Glue is also used to bond joinings that will be additionally strengthened with dowels or screws. You follow the same steps for the actual gluing.

Joining with dowels: Dowels are added into wood joints for greater strength than you would have with glue alone. They are also used in many toys as the main means of holding one part to the next, as axles for wheels, to make parts that can bend or rotate, and instead of nails or screws. The most important thing to do when making a dowel joint of any sort is to drill accurate holes. To mark the holes, place the two sections to be joined right next to each other. Check the measurements and mark each spot with an awl. Line them up to see that they are the same. As you drill the holes, test with the square to make them perfectly straight. If you have a vise, you may also want to try drilling with the wood held vertically and the drill held horizontally. Try it on scrap beforehand.

Use a piece of tape, a block, or a bit gauge to drill to the required depth when you are making holes that only go partway into the wood. For the first dowel joints that you make, it will be best to work with practice parts, both to see how the process works and to select the right size drill bit to fit the dowel. Generally, you choose the bit that is the same size as the dowel's diameter. It's better when the dowel is slightly too big as it can be sanded down and the glue won't fill it in if the hole is too large.

The dowels are cut to the right length with a saw. In projects, cut them to the specified length. For your own plans, cut the dowels to fit. When you are placing a short dowel partway into two sides of a joint, it should be about ⅛" less than the depth of the hole so that you're sure there is room for it to fit in place as the two parts are put together. For dowels that go straight through one or more sections, you can make the dowel to fit, or slightly longer as you can always sand it down.

The same procedure is followed in gluing as for gluing any two parts together. The dowel is very lightly covered with glue and fitted into one hole; then, both surfaces are covered with glue, fitted together around the dowel, and clamped as usual.

For dowels that are to go through parts that will move, such as axles, or are to join two parts that will bend and move, you drill a clearance hole for the dowel, large enough to permit it to turn. One drill bit a size larger may not be sufficient, but you can test it on scrap. You want the axle, or free-moving dowel, to turn easily without making the hole so large that it is really loose. Once the dowel is threaded through the hole, in the case of an axle, you fit on the wheels. In the toys shown, the wheels are all wood, so that the dowels are fitted to the same diameter as their holes. The wheels are glued on when the dowel is in place.

For a free-moving joint, as in the Dachshund (see page 116), you make a variation of what is known in woodworking as a mortise and tenon joint. Basically, for toys, the object of this joining is that one part can swivel on the other as it is held by a dowel. The two opposing parts are cut from one piece of wood in what looks something like a large jigsaw puzzle shape. One side of the wood has a protruding tab shape, and the other naturally has the concave matching half. Each side is sanded until smooth and somewhat smaller than it was to allow room to move. The two halves are held about ⅜" apart as you mark the holes. On the top and bottom of the concave piece, you drill a hole which fits the dowel closely. Through the tab shape, you drill a hole that is up to ⅛″ larger than the dowel so that this part can move freely on the dowel. Then, you glue the parts after you have the dowel threaded through the top, bottom, and the tab. The glue is hard to get on in this position because you must slide the dowel through all the sections first. Work from the top and slide the dowel down toward the bottom a little and put a small amount of glue into the top hole. Slide the dowel up and through it, just far enough to add some glue into the bottom hole from the bottom. Never put any glue on the dowel itself. The glue should be kept off the center area of the dowel as you slide it back into place. That's why you use just enough glue to secure it, adding it in from the top and bottom.

Joints: There are many different ways in which you can prepare the edges of the wood to make a sturdy joint. This is the name for any coming together of two parts. You've already become familiar with the basic joint, where you bring two flat edges together in what is called a butt joint,

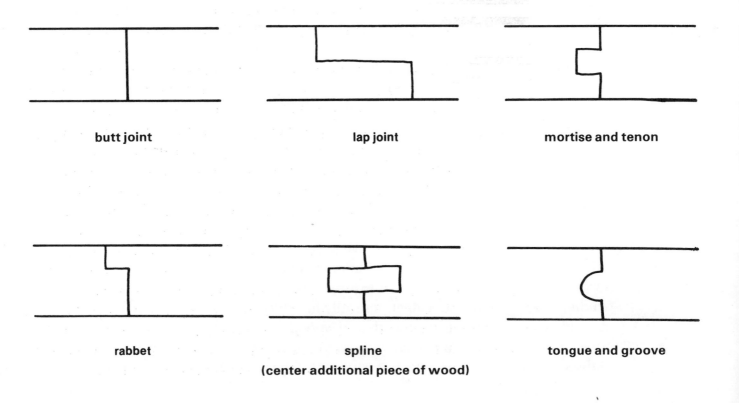

butt joint   **lap joint**   **mortise and tenon**

rabbet   **spline**   **tongue and groove**
(center additional piece of wood)

and the dowel joint, in which the flat edges have short lengths of dowel added into them for strength.

The other types of joints, common in woodworking, are not that widely used in toy making. These are the lap joint, mortise and tenon, rabbet, spline, and tongue and groove. They are most easily understood by looking at the diagram shown. The joints are prepared beforehand, often with sophisticated edging tools which can create the needed forms, or with chisels by hand. For this reason, they are usually too complex for making the simple constructions that best suit wooden toys. It is useful to know what they are, especially since they can be simplified and adapted, as was shown in the swivel joint.

Driving screws: Driving screws is simple when you make the right preparations. For small screws in pine or other softwoods, you can mark the spot with an awl, making a small depression, as a starter hole. Then, you use the right size screwdriver and set the screw in place.

For longer screws, or when you are working with hardwood, you drill a hole to fit the screw, called a pilot hole. In many cases this is a composite hole, made in three steps. First, drill a hole that is the same width and length as the plain, unthreaded top half of the shank. Second, drill a slightly smaller hole in the bottom of the first that is the same depth as the threaded bottom of the screw. Then, when you're using flathead screws, you open out the top of the hole to fit the top in a step called countersinking. For other types of screws which remain on the surface, this is unnecessary. There are special countersink bits made for this job.

For medium-sized screws, you can often drill just the pilot hole, the same size as the bottom of the screw and the same depth. If you rub a little paraffin on the screw, it will go in more easily. When you make pilot holes and use the right size screwdriver, you'll never have the problems of wearing off the slot in the screw or breaking the wood as it goes in.

To simulate the effect of dowel joinings, to make screws look like pegs, you make a plug with a short length of dowel. The first hole is made the same size as the head of the screw, ½" deep. Then, you make the pilot holes in the bottom of that hole. Set the screw as usual. Cut a ⁷⁄₁₆" length of dowel the same diameter as the screwhead and glue it into the hole. Sand the top smooth, so that the plug is the same level as the surface after the glue has dried.

Driving nails: Nails should be used sparingly, if at all, in making toys; they don't hold as well as other fastenings and can be dangerous if they happen to become exposed when a toy is in use. As for all joints in toys, you'll find it better to glue the parts together beforehand.

When you do use nails, they are ideally hammered in at a slight angle. This is called toeing in. It allows the nail to hold better. It takes a bit of practice, as once a nail bends from a mistaken hit, it can't be straightened correctly. Often a nail that looks straight on the surface is still bent inside the wood. Take out bent nails and start with new ones.

Hinges: When metal hinges are used, it's most important to mark carefully the spots for the screws that hold the hinges in place. Place the hinge on the part and mark through its holes with a pencil. Then drill pilot holes for the screws on the marks.

Making wheels: Many wooden toys have wheels. They seem to look best when the wheels are made out of wood and complement the natural textures of the toy itself. There are many types of wooden wheels that you can make. If you prefer, you can buy rubber wheels, and entire axle assemblies. In well-supplied woodcraft stores you may also find wooden wheels, which are very handy and useful to have.

The best type of wheel that you can make is cut from a large dowel. When you make wheels, you can have all sorts of sizes and types, as you do them yourself to suit the toy you are making. You can use dowels with a diameter of 1" up to 3" for wheels of these diameters. With the dowel clamped in place, saw off sections of about ½" for smaller wheels and up to ¾" for the larger sizes. Round off the edges with sandpaper or a file, and sand smooth. The center hole should be carefully marked and drilled according to the axle you will use. Dowel axles are very effective; you drill a hole that is the same diameter as the axle when the axles move and the wheels are fixed in place on them. It's better to sand down the end of the axle a bit if it's too large for the wheel hole than to try to glue a wheel in place on a small axle.

To glue the wheels on an axle, you glue and let dry. Then, using the smallest dowel you can find, usually $\frac{3}{16}$", you make a spear to hold it in place. Use the same size drill bit and drill a hole into the wheel from its edge to the depth of the center hole, with the axle dowel now in place. Glue the dowel and slip it into the hole. Cut it off right at the wheel and sand smooth. For wheels that will be placed once a dowel axle has been threaded into a clearance hole in the toy (as is the case with the placement of the second wheel in many projects), you follow the same steps to secure the second wheel that you followed for the first. But you repeat them for the second wheel after the axle is placed in the toy. Thus the entire wheel assembly is secured in the clearance hole. The hole is larger in diameter than the axle so that the axle can turn.

When you want to have fixed axles with rotating wheels, you glue the axles in place in the toy, making them longer than you would for fixed wheels, which are usually flush with the axle end. Before you put it on the axle, two $\frac{3}{16}$" holes are drilled about $\frac{3}{8}$" in from the end of each one. Then, you glue the axle into the toy. Next, drill clearance holes that are $\frac{1}{8}$" larger than the axle-rod diameter in the wheels and slip the wheel onto the axle. Make a $\frac{3}{16}$" dowel peg and slip it into the drilled $\frac{3}{16}$" hole in the axle. The dowel peg should extend out past the hole for at least $\frac{1}{8}$" on either side to hold the wheel on the axle. You can cut off the dowel after it is in place, or precut it, using the diameter of the axle dowel as a guide in cutting the right length, which should be that diameter plus $\frac{1}{4}$".

Other wheel possibilities are to cut wider sections from dowelling and not smooth the edge round, for the look of big wheels. It's possible to cut wheels from lengths of wood, but it is hard to get a really round circle unless you buy a circle cutter, used with a power drill. Large wooden beads or wooden balls through which you can drill holes are quite suitable for many toys and are easy to find in craft supply stores.

Rounding edges and corners: For a finished edging, the sharp corners left when you cut out a piece of wood are smoothed off. The extent of the smoothing, or rounding, depends on the toy itself and the look you want to create. In most cases, the edges are simply sanded down, so that they are very slightly round and nice to the touch. This type of sanding is done just for smoothing, not to change the appearance of the shape. Even squared edges should be lightly sanded.

Chamfering is the slicing off of the edge corner on a forty-five degree angle. For softwoods, you can often accomplish this with sandpaper on a block. For hardwoods and precise chamfering, you use a plane, which shaves off the wood neatly. A beveled edge is also made with a plane. It is done on the same angle as a chamfer, but the entire corner is removed.

For a really round edge, the corner can be cut off as for a chamfer and then sanded smooth until it takes on a round look. This is usually done with a plane or a surform and sandpaper.

Shaping: Shaping is done to change the form of a section of wood that is cut out with a saw. First, the basic shape is made, using the saw to accomplish as much of the shaping as possible. Then, the medium grades of sandpaper are used to further define the shape. You'll find that this can be a very effective way to add different kinds of shapes into your toys. The sandpaper works more rapidly than might be expected and can create all kinds of forms that have some of the sculptural aspects of carved wood. As wood carving is an art, which uses its own set of tools, the sanding method is a nice alternative. Once you have the shape that you want, you switch to fine papers to smooth the surface. When you shape with sandpaper, you still try to go with the grain as much as possible to avoid a lot of extra sanding with fine paper for a smooth finished surface.

5
Finishing Techniques

Once your toy is complete, you can finish it in many ways. The choice depends on the type of effect that you want to create. All of the finishing techniques are done when the toy is completely assembled. That's why it's important to do the initial sanding before the parts are put together. A light sanding with the finest paper is done after the toy is whole to remove any marks that gathered on the surface as you made it.

While you do the last sanding, you can look at all of the joinings to be sure that there is no extra glue or other foreign matter left on the surface. If there is, carefully remove it and sand smooth. If you have trouble reaching any tight areas that need some sanding, use an emery board, or cut thin strips of sandpaper and stiffen them by gluing to a thin slat of wood. For any touch-up sanding, finish the area with the finest grade paper so that the entire surface of the toy is uniform.

Next you decide which type of finish you want. There are as many mixtures and methods as there are woodworkers. You have several general types to choose among. For a natural wood beauty that lasts, you can use any one of a number of clear finishes.

Oil: One of the easiest to do, and most suitable when you don't want the toy to have a shiny look, is an oiled finish. Linseed oil is used for this, and it dries to a neat and nonoily surface. You can apply the oil with a soft, lint-free cloth pad or a new paintbrush. The oil penetrates better when you mix it with an equal amount of turpentine and brush on a thin coat. As soon as you've done this, wipe off the extra oil with a soft cloth. You can leave it as is, or add up to three coats, following the same procedure. When you build up several coats, allowing each to dry thoroughly, you can buff the surface with a soft cloth and you'll get a nice sheen. The surface can be touched up whenever you like. You'll find that as you add any finish to wood, the grain becomes more clearly defined and the color darkens slightly. The oil finish does this to a lesser extent than many, but it does change somewhat.

Wax: A wax finish is soft and attractive. To wax, you can buy one of the many types of wax available. If you want to keep the same color, use clear wax. To change the hue, there are wax stains, which polish in some added shades. For the most part, the plain wax looks best. It is applied with a soft cloth and left on for about an hour and a half. Then you wipe down the surface with a cloth. You can add one or two more coats this way, or stop at one and buff with a clean cloth. The more coats you add, the shinier a surface you can make by buffing.

Both oil and wax will penetrate more if you apply them in a slightly warm room. This is particularly true of waxes, which can be hard to even get out of the can when they are cold.

As you finish the toys, remember that they are going to be used by children. Since you never know how they will be played with, it's best to put on as safe a finish as you can. Oil and wax finishes are good for this reason. Most of each is wiped off and the rest penetrates the wood, so that there is little or no residue left behind.

Shellac, polyurethane, and varnish: When you want to make a shiny, clear finish, you can use white shellac, clear polyurethane, or varnish. When you buy any type of paint or finish, make sure that it is safe for use on articles that will be handled by children. For your safety, use the necessary thinners and such in well-ventilated rooms and protect your hands with gloves.

You can brush on a smooth surface with any of the clear shellacs and varnishes as long as the wood you are painting has a good, smoothly sanded surface to begin with. You'll discover that wood that is not well sanded actually looks worse once it has been covered. If sanding is not one of your strong points, the oil and wax finishes are for you.

Any of these paint-on finishes must be applied to a clean, smooth surface. White shellac, thinned with denatured alcohol for the first coat; polyurethane, which is a type of plastic varnish and comes in gloss, semigloss, and satin finishes; clear lacquer; and varnish, also thinned with thinner, will produce a good finish. You carefully apply them with a clean brush and allow to dry thoroughly. Then, sand lightly, or rub with steel wool, wipe off all dust with a clean lint-free cloth, and brush on another coat. For a final coat, you sand lightly after the previous one is dry, and add one more coat. As you work with these, dip the brush into the can so that only the lower parts of the bristles get wet. Try not to wipe the brush across the top of the can if you can avoid it, as this common habit adds air to the brush. For a good finish, air bubbles are definitely not wanted. Try to brush each area only once during each coat since you can make the finish too thick with brushing on top of a just completed stroke. As you complete a coat, look over the toy carefully so that you can cover any spots you missed right away. For polyurethane especially, the sanding between coats is an essential step. When it is added on top of an unsanded coat, it builds up into a layer that is thick enough to peel off.

When you complete the final coat, clean your brushes well and let the toy dry. As you are working, the brush can be allowed to stand temporarily on its bristles, but you should not store them in this manner, or ever let them sit for hours. The bristles will become permanently bent and won't be very useful.

Paint: Toys painted in colors can be an interesting contrast to those in natural hues. Whenever you plan to paint a toy, it should have the same careful preparation as for a clear finish. Paint will hide a fair number of minor flaws, but painted toys look best when they have a high gloss, which only happens on smooth wood.

Cheerful lacquers and enamels produce a shiny surface. You should also buy a small amount of wood primer for the first coat. Whichever type of paint and primer you plan to use, make absolutely sure of the fact that they do not contain any lead. Although lead-based paints are becoming increasingly rare, they do exist and should never be used for things that children will handle.

The first coat of primer is sanded down once it is completely dry. Then you brush on the first layer of color. Paint carefully, trying to get the surface as even as you can. Let the paint dry and sand it down with fine sandpaper. The third coat is then applied and allowed to dry. For a really high gloss you may want to add one more coat of paint. If so, sand first and then paint. The sanding between coats gives the paint enough of a texture that following coats can adhere properly and should not be omitted.

Stain: To change the color of wood without obscuring the grain, wood stains are used. There are many different types, based on oil, water, or alcohol. They are applied in the same manner as shellacs and varnishes, with the exception that the dry stains are often waxed for additional sheen. You'll find that the stains come out a good deal darker than you might think, so you should choose a shade that is a little lighter than the one you want. As many stains are intended to give pine the look of more exotic woods, they have names like honey maple. There are also stains that add an actual color, although the grain of the wood can still be seen.

Whatever type of finish you decide to use, once the last application has dried and been buffed to a nice soft sheen, if needed, the toy is done. As you complete your first toy and have a chance to see how well it has turned out, you'll understand why making wooden toys is such a gratifying experience.

6

The Toys: Plans and Patterns

These designs will introduce you to the enjoyment you'll experience making attractive, functional wooden toys. If one of these toys is the first thing that you will make out of wood, relax and let the tools do the work—the results are sure to please.

Each toy shown is made with the basic set of hand tools and equipment that can easily be gathered in a comfortable work area. As you begin a toy, make a list of the required wood and check off each piece as you get it, so that you've got everything you need when you start.

Apart from the drying time of glue and finishes, many of the toys can be completed in a matter of hours. The group under Quick Toys can be accomplished even sooner. For your first project, it's sometimes more gratifying when you make something in a relatively short time. You'll see tangible proof of your newly developing skills and be inspired to go on to another toy. All of these toys can be made with fundamental techniques by a beginning woodworker.

Quick Toys

These quick toys are just that—you can make them up fast, and they are good stocking stuffers or party favors. You'll enjoy making them, and perhaps thinking up some of your own to add to the collection. They can be made out of small bits and pieces, odds and ends, making use of all of the wood and parts that you have on hand.

The toys are basic enough that you can create them by following the diagrams without further explanation.

For the tops, use assorted dowels and wheels as shown.

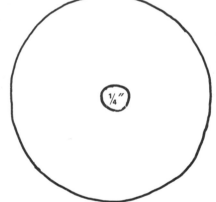

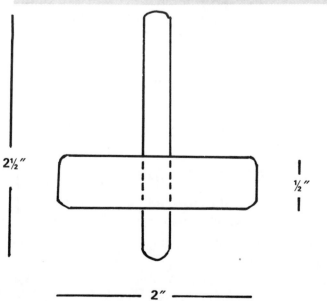

Little people and animal friends, simply cut from scrap lumber, can be decorated with waterproof fine line markers as desired.

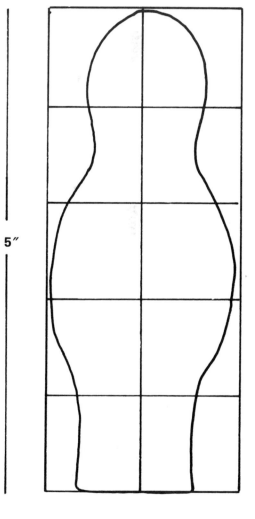

5″

2″

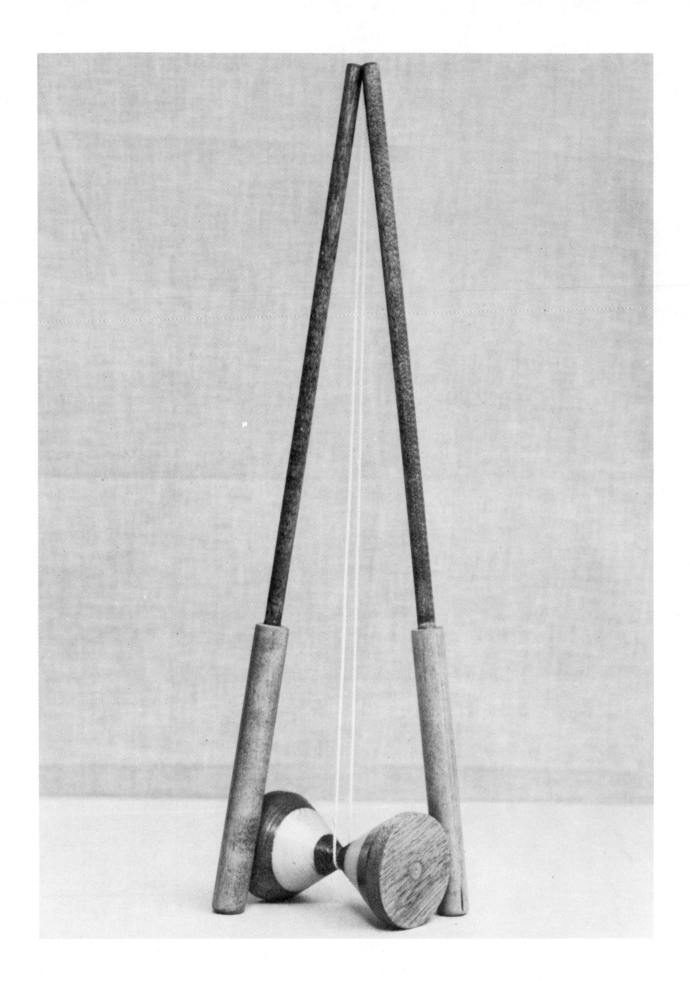

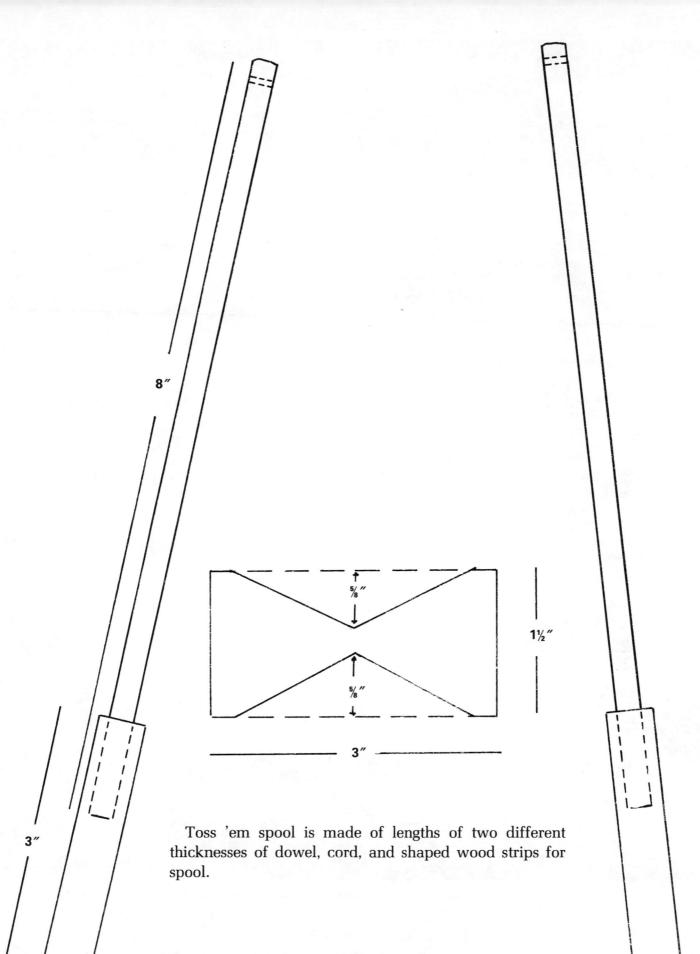

8″

3″

⅝″

1½″

⅝″

3″

Toss 'em spool is made of lengths of two different thicknesses of dowel, cord, and shaped wood strips for spool.

69

Jointed bear is made of scraps of thin wood, in a form
that is adaptable to many animals, as shown. Joints are
held with machine screws. Top hole is clearance, bottom
to fit. Strings can be added to make it into a marionette.

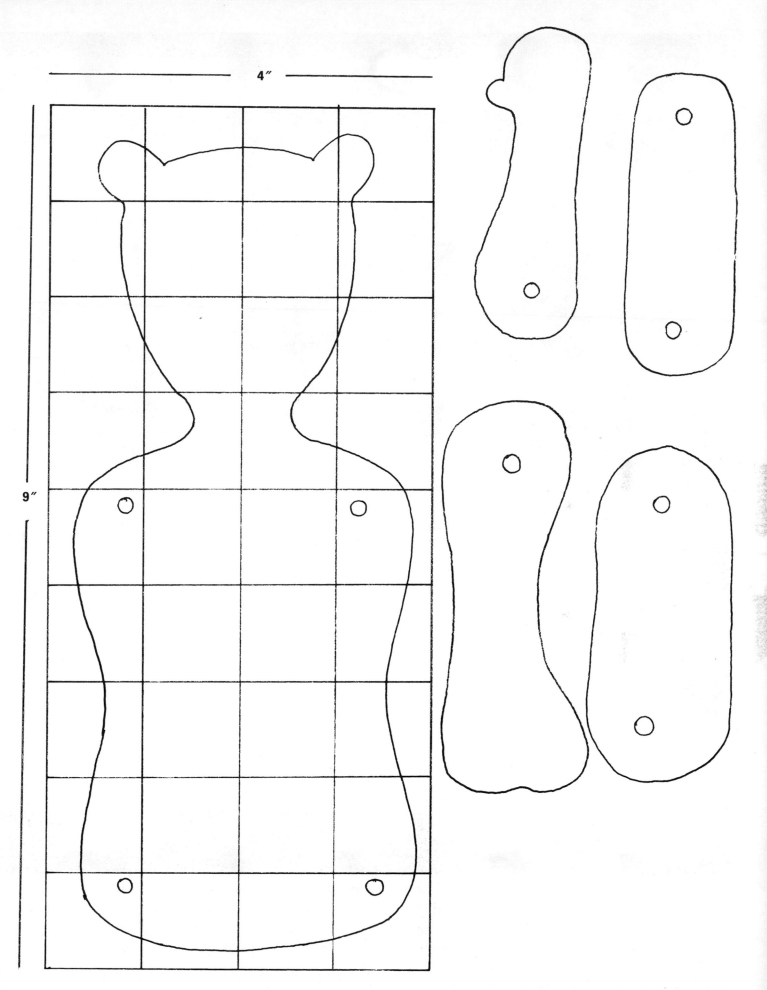

4"

9"

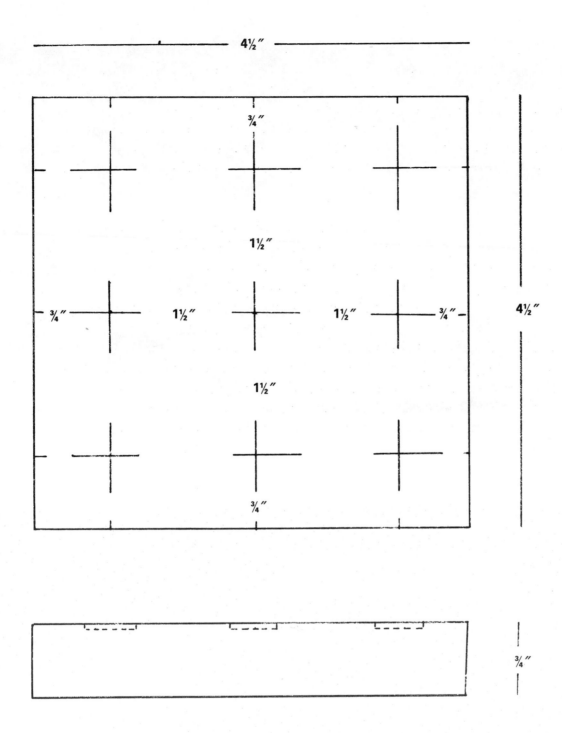

Ticktacktoe set is made of scrap lumber and wooden balls as shown.

Quick toys are fun to do, and they can be finished with a simple coat of linseed oil or wax, or any other finish that you like.

Paddle Tug Boat

The paddle boat, which moves as its four-surfaced paddle turns in the water, is a time-honored toy. This tug is one of the variations you can make, all of which are based on a similarly shaped body and paddle design. To make one, you'll need:

1 length of clear pine, ¾″ × 4¾″ × 10¾″
1 length of clear pine, ¾″ × 2″ × 4″
2 lengths of white pine, ⅜″ × 2″ × 3″
1 dowel, 1⅜″ diameter
1 dowel, ½″ diameter
1 dowel, ¼″ diameter
1 dowel, ⅛″ diameter
Several ¼″ wide rubber bands

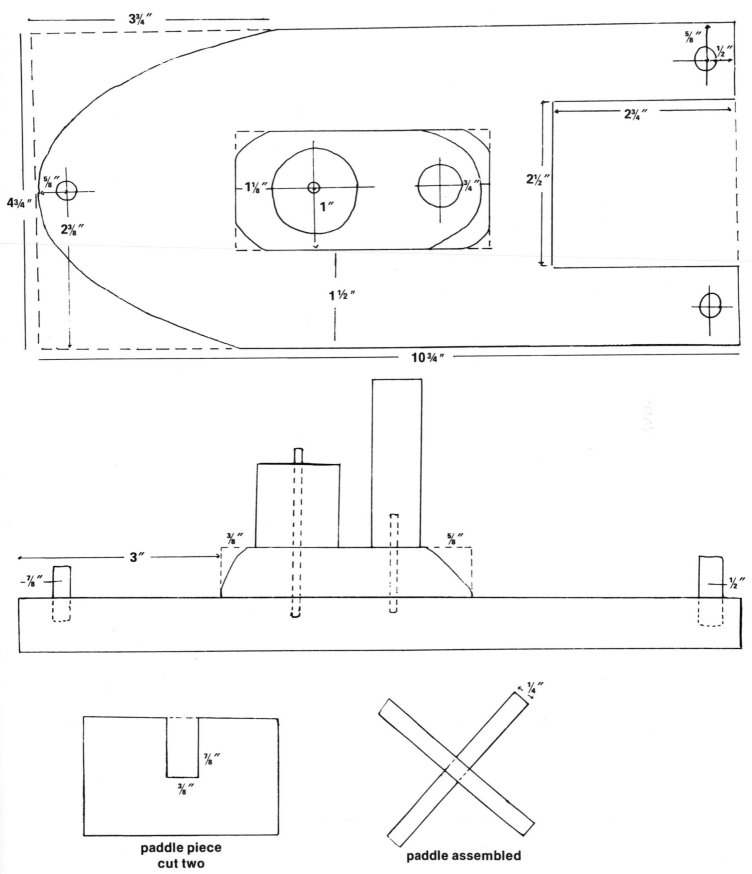

**paddle piece
cut two**

paddle assembled

Trace and enlarge pattern parts.

Sand lengths of wood on wide surfaces, as it's easier than when the parts are cut out.

Transfer hull body pattern to large plank, cabin to 4″ length, and notches to two 3″ lengths for paddle as shown in diagram.

Cut out hull and cabin. Sand to shape.

Cut notches in paddle parts. Sand only to smooth.

Glue hull to cabin. Let dry.

Glue paddle parts after trying the notches by sliding them together to check their fit. Let dry.

Cut one 1¼″ length of the 1⅜″ dowel. Drill one ⅜″ hole through the side, as shown, for window.

Glue windowed dowel to cabin, using ⅛″ dowel peg, into a ½″ deep, ⅛″ blind hole in cabin top and dowel bottom. Let dry. Add ⅛″ dowel at top of windowed dowel as shown.

Cut one 3″ length of the ½″ diameter dowel. Drill one ½″ diameter hole through cabin into body, ⅞″ deep, as indicated.

Fit 3″ dowel into hole, sanding if needed. Glue in place for smokestack. Let dry.

Cut three 1½″ lengths of ¼″ diameter dowel.

Drill three ¼″ diameter blind holes in body as marked, each ½″ deep, for bowline post and two paddle holders at rear.

Glue dowels in three holes, sanding to thin if needed to fit. Let dry.

Do final light sanding of all parts to remove pattern markings or other marks.

Finish with two coats of polyurethane, sanding lightly between first and second. Allow to dry thoroughly.

Slip one rubber band around the paddle and loop its ends around the two paddle posts. Wind it up and it will ride along the water in bath or pool.

Seaplane

To make this double-winged seaplane, you'll need:

1 length of pine, 1½" × 2½" × 10", for body
2 lengths of pine, ⅝" × 1½" × 4", for pontoons
1 1ength of pine, ¼" × 1½" × 24", for wings and tail
1 dowel, ¼" diameter
1 wooden ball, 1" diameter

Trace all pattern parts.
Transfer outlines onto appropriate lengths of wood.
Cut out one body, two pontoons, two wings, and one tail.

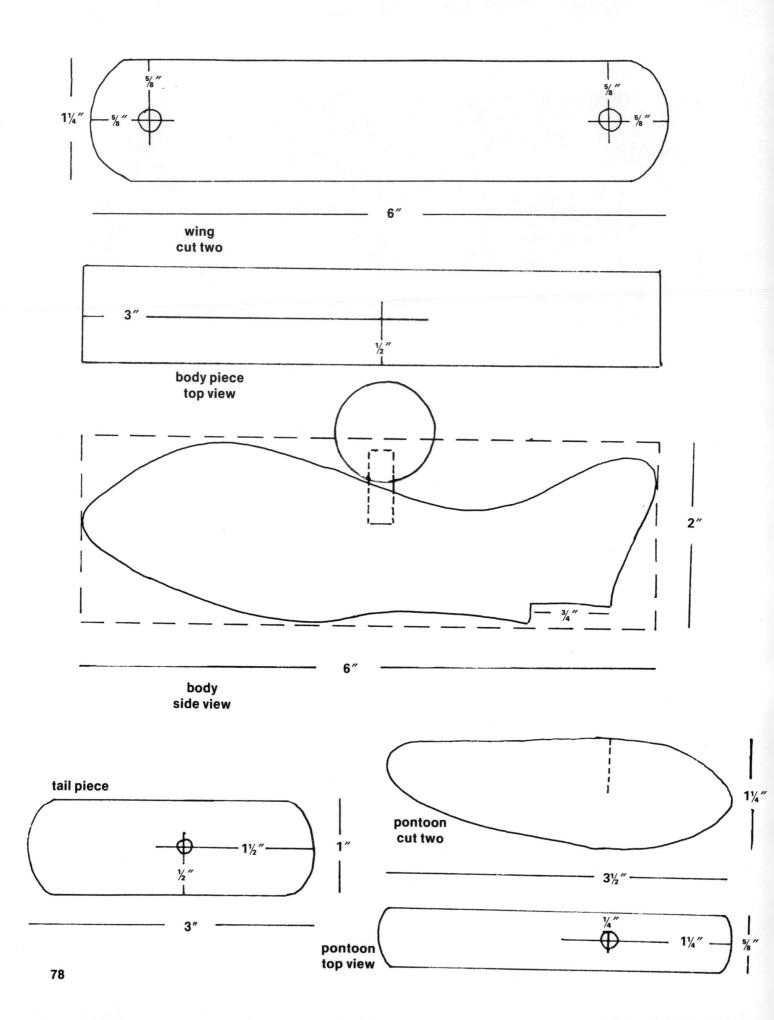

5/8"

5/8"

1¼" 5/8"

5/8"

6"

**wing
cut two**

3"

½"

**body piece
top view**

2"

6"

¾"

**body
side view**

tail piece

1½"

½"

1"

**pontoon
cut two**

1¼"

3½"

**pontoon
top view**

¼"

1¼"

5/8"

3"

78

Mark for holes at each wing tip with an awl, which will help start the drilling.

Drill ¼" holes on wings as indicated.

Mark and drill same size holes ½" deep, called blind holes, in top center of each pontoon and into body for ball as shown.

Sand all parts smooth.

Cut two 4½" lengths of dowel.

Glue one dowel into top of first pontoon, the other into top of second. Let dry. Drill hole to fit into ball; cut ¼" dowel and glue pilot in place.

Glue lower wing to body as shown, centering wing as indicated on wing pattern part. Let dry.

Glue tail to slight incision in lower back of body. Let dry.

Slip dowels on pontoons into lower wing at holes. Sand the dowels, if needed, to fit into holes.

Position upper wing on dowels and glue in place. Let dry.

Sand tops of wing to make dowel ends flush.

Do final sanding.

Finish with one part white shellac and one part denatured alcohol. Let dry. Sand lightly.

Apply second coat of shellac full strength if it is new, or in above proportions if it has been opened and used before.

If you like the Sopwith Camel type of biplane, you can make one following the same pattern. The pontoons are replaced with a standard wheel assembly, and a propeller is added to the nose of the plane. (For propeller see Whimmy Diddle p. 114.)

Pull Duck

Pull toys made in natural wood, with its unique texture in view, seem to be special favorites of children of all ages. They're actually easy to make and you'll enjoy putting bird and animal shapes on wheels to delight a child. The pull duck is a good shape to start with as it's not hard to cut out. You'll need:

1 length of pine, ¾″ × 9½″ × 10″
1 dowel, ¼″ diameter
4 round wooden beads, 1¾″ diameter, for wheels
1 round wooden bead, 1″ diameter
1 length of cord, twine, or lightweight rope, 2′

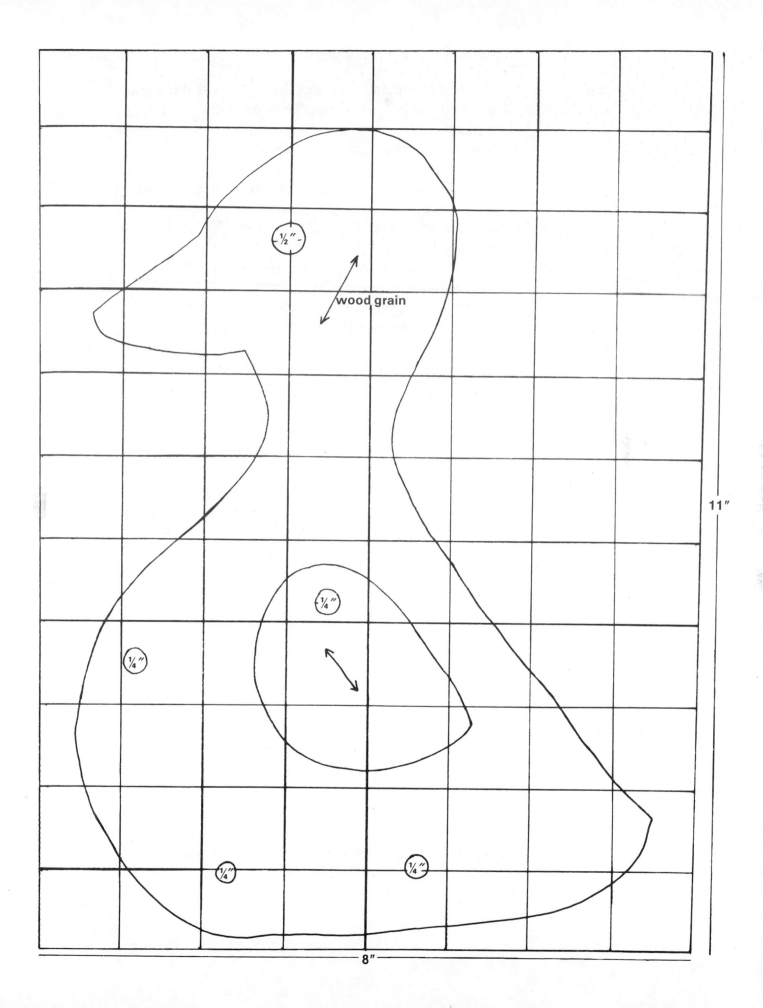

½″

wood grain

¼″

¼″

¼″

¼″

11″

8″

Trace and enlarge pattern. Lay on wood with grain slightly on the bias as shown. Transfer outlines with carbon paper.

Cut out the shape with a coping saw.

Drill two ⅜" diameter holes for axles as marked.

Drill one ¼" diameter hole for eye and one in same diameter in body for pull cord as shown.

Cut one ¾" length of ¼" diameter dowel. Glue into eye space. Let dry.

Sand eye dowel flush, and sand all smooth without rounding edges.

Cut two 4" lengths of ¼" diameter dowel for axles.

Glue one large bead flush with end of axle; repeat. Let dry.

Slip axles into place, glue one large bead on each. Let dry.

Sand outer bead surfaces at axles smooth and even.

Finish as desired to protect the wood surface.

Tie the cord into hole, knot 1" diameter bead on end, and the pull duck is ready to roll.

For added dimension, you can add wings to the pull duck. Trace the wing pattern, cut two wings from the scrap left when you cut out the duck. Sand smooth. Drill one ¼" diameter hole as shown in each wing. Cut one 2¼" length of ¼" diameter dowel. Glue one wing to the dowel as shown. Let dry. Drill one ⅜" hole in body as marked. Slip in dowel, position second wing as shown, and glue. Let dry.

This type of shape-on-wheels pattern is one of the most versatile that you can use to create wooden toys. Children are constantly in motion, and they seem to prefer their toys that way. You'll find that all sorts of forms, shapes, and sizes are well suited to the basic concept. When you are practiced at contour cutting, they can be completed in good time and they make terrific gifts.

Saw-Carved Helicopter

This redwood helicopter is an example of shaping with a coping saw and sandpaper to create a carved effect. Redwood is excellent for this type of work, as it is softer than pine and easy to shape. You will have equally good finished results if you use clear pine, but they may take a little longer to achieve. You'll need:

1 length of 2 × 4 redwood or pine, 1½″ × 3½″ × 10″
1 dowel, ³⁄₁₆″ diameter

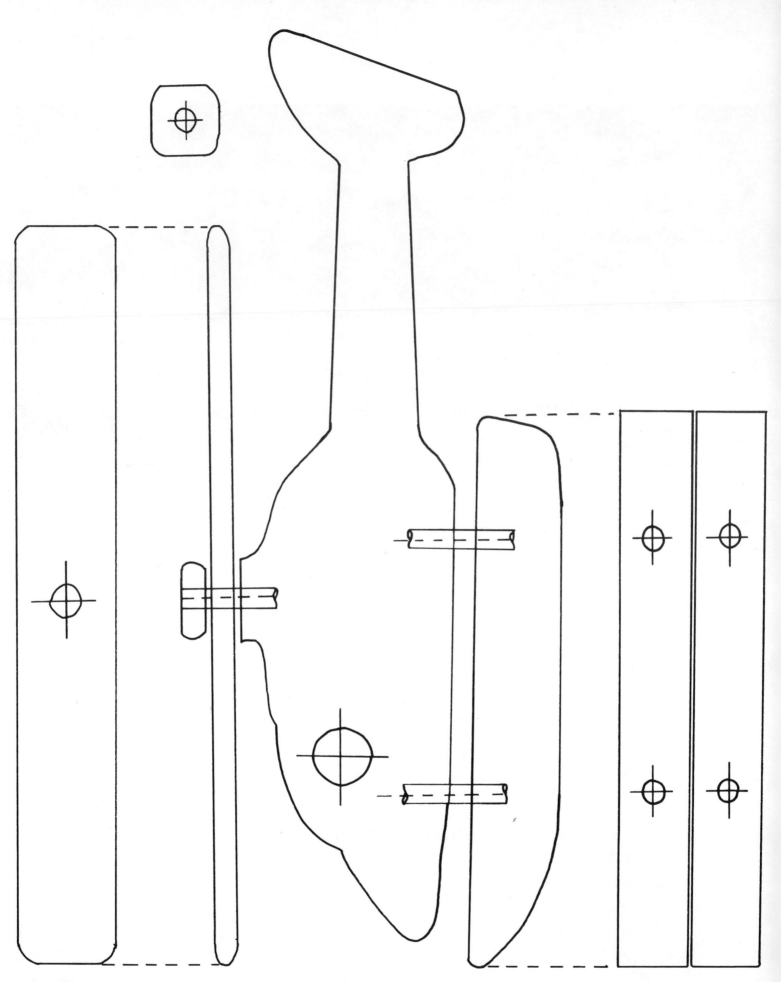

Trace pattern, mark on wood in layout shown.

Cut out pontoon section, then propeller and holding button, body last, using coping saw.

Cut pontoon section in half lengthwise from short edge as shown.

Mark top of body section for side shaping.

Cut side shaping in body with coping saw.

Mark and drill ⅝″ hole, as indicated, in body for window.

Drill 3/16″ diameter blind hole ½″ deep in top for propeller.

Drill four 3/16″ diameter blind holes ½″ deep at bottom of body as indicated.

Sand body to shape, rounding all edges; then sand smooth.

Cut five 1¼″ lengths of 3/16″ diameter dowel.

Mark and drill two 3/16″ blind holes ⅜″ deep in each pontoon as shown.

Sand pontoons, rounding edges and then smoothing.

Mark and drill one ¼″ diameter hole in propeller.

Sand propeller, rounding. Sand smooth.

Mark and drill one 3/16″ diameter hole in top button as shown.

Sand, rounding and then smoothing.

With five lengths of 1¼″ long dowel, glue one into blind hole at top body, one each into blind holes in each pontoon. Let dry.

Place propeller onto dowel shaft at top, spin to check clearance.

Carefully glue top button over propeller on dowel shaft. Make sure the glue does not seep down and glue the propeller still. Rotate to check. Let dry.

Glue pontoons to body, four dowels at bottom, placing each into one hole in the lower body of the helicopter. Let dry.

Finish as desired.

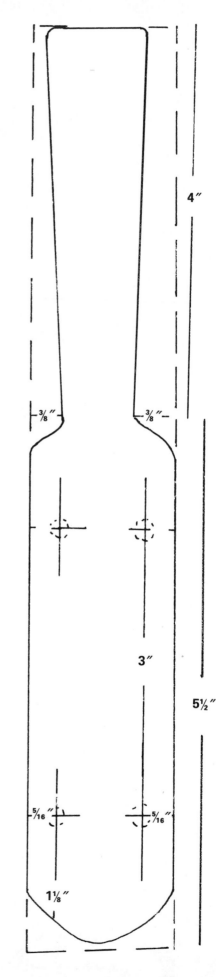

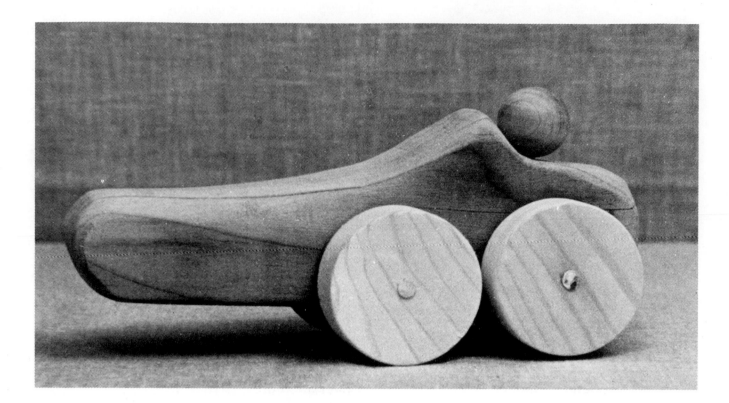

Torpedo Race Car

To make this speedy-looking torpedo racer, you'll need:

1 length of redwood, 1¾″ × 3½″ × 9″
1 dowel, ⅜″ diameter
1 dowel, 2″ diameter, or 4 wheels, 2″ diameter, ¾″ thick
1 wooden ball, 1″ diameter, for passenger

Trace and enlarge pattern.
Transfer outlines onto the wood.
Cut out the shape with a coping saw.

Use surform and sandpaper, or sandpaper alone, to shape and smooth top, front, bottom, and back as indicated.

Mark body with awl for holes, drill each with ⅝″ diameter bit. Following diagram, drill for passenger dowel, assemble, and glue in hole drilled to fit.

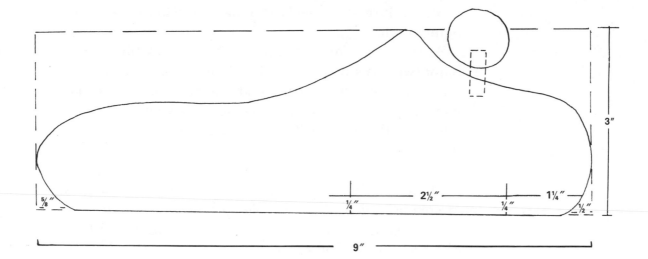

Cut four ¾″ thick segments of the 2″ diameter dowel with a handsaw. Sand cuts smooth, chamfer edges.

Mark each wheel in exact center with awl, drill a ⅜″ hole in each. For bought wheels, choose a dowel that fits the center hole or enlarge it to ⅜″ if it is smaller.

Cut two 3¼″ lengths of the ⅜″ diameter dowel.

Glue one length of dowel to one wheel, flush with its side. Repeat with second length of dowel, into another wheel. Let dry.

Slip one wheel and dowel axle into front hole in body. Place third wheel on dowel and glue in place, flush with side. Let dry. Repeat for rear axle and fourth wheel. Let dry.

Do final sanding with special attention to the outer wheels and axle ends in their centers.

Finish with three coats of a high-gloss clear enamel, lacquer, or polyurethane, sanding with very fine paper after the first two coats are dry. Do not try to put more than one coat in the space behind each wheel. As each coat dries, carefully turn the wheels to make sure the axle is not painted still.

An alternate plan, if you want a really sleek finish, is to paint two coats before the wheels are in place. To follow this procedure, support the body on two dowels so that you can paint the bottom; take extra care when gluing the wheels so that you don't mar the finish or get any glue on it.

Many simple but effective car, van and truck shapes are made on the same principles as this race car. The major part is the body, with two dowel rod axles and four suitable wheels. You can use the same dowel and wheel assembly for cars made out of the same size wood up to a $1\frac{3}{4}'' \times 3\frac{1}{2}'' \times 10''$. The sedan, speedy racer, bug, and bus shown are examples of this type of construction. Follow the same steps, checking with the photograph and using the diagram for each car you want to make. The finish is up to you—for less rakish-looking cars like these, a simple oil or wax finish is quite appealing.

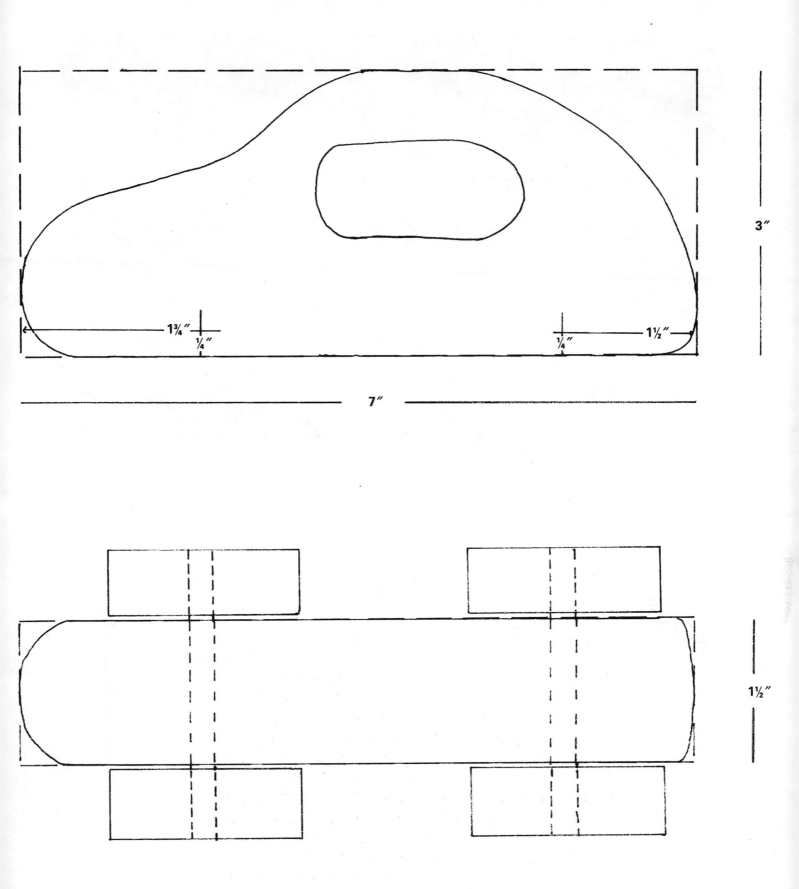

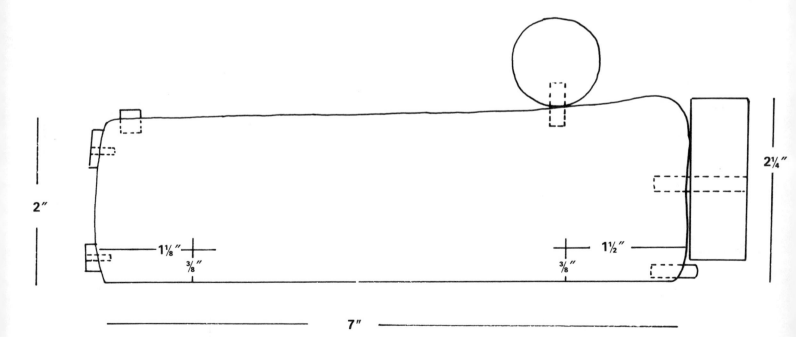

2″

2¼″

1⅛″

3/8″

1½″

3/8″

7″

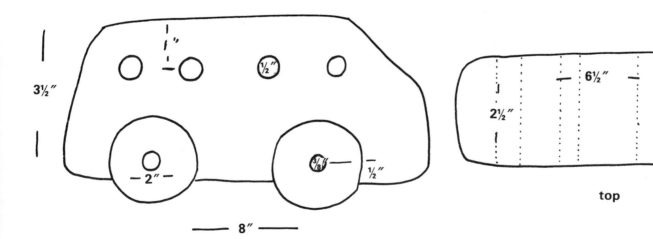

6½″

3½″

½″

¾″

2″

3/8″

½″

8″

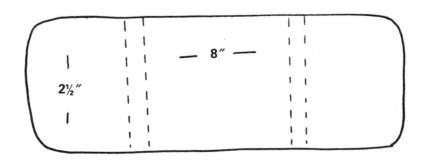

6½″

2½″

top

2½″

8″

bottom

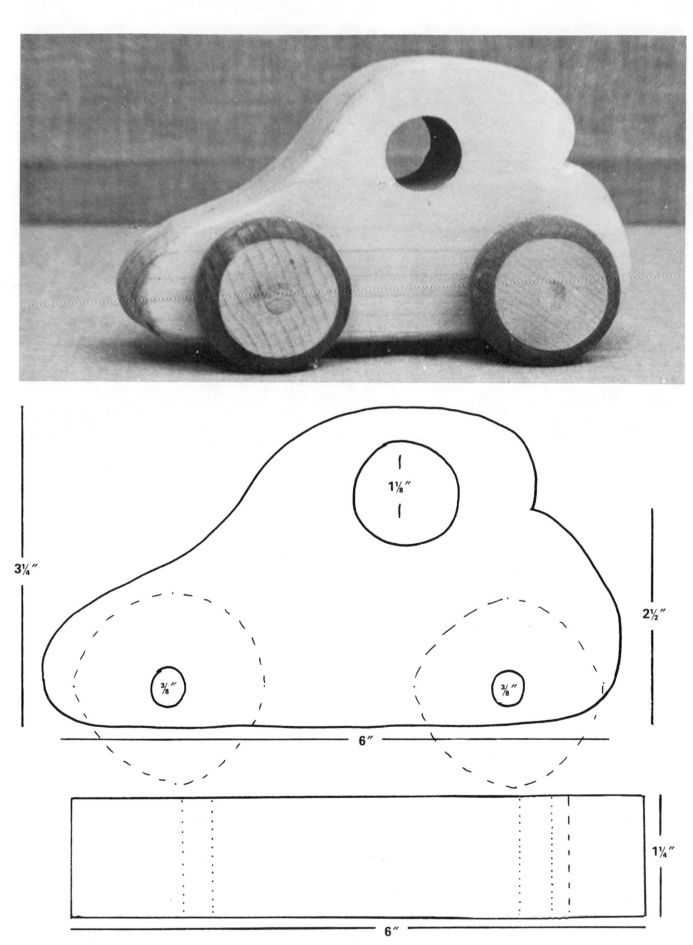

3¼″

1⅛″

2½″

3/8″   3/8″

6″

1¼″

6″

92   **bottom view**

Red Woodie

This red woodie is a more complex version of the basic car design. It is made out of a piece of redwood two by four detailed with dowels of various thicknesses. You can use pine, cedar, or any softwood that's readily available. You'll need:

1 length of redwood, 1½″ × 3½″ × 6½″, for body and bumper
1 dowel, 2″ diameter, for five wheels (or 5 bought wheels, axle dowel sized to fit the holes)
1 dowel, ½″ diameter, for headlights
1 dowel, ¼″ diameter, for axles
1 dowel, ³⁄₁₆″ diameter for bumper rivets and tail pipe

Trace the full-sized pattern.

Transfer onto the redwood with carbon paper and a pencil.

Cut it out with a coping saw, saving scraps. Redwood is a pleasure to cut, as it's softer than pine.

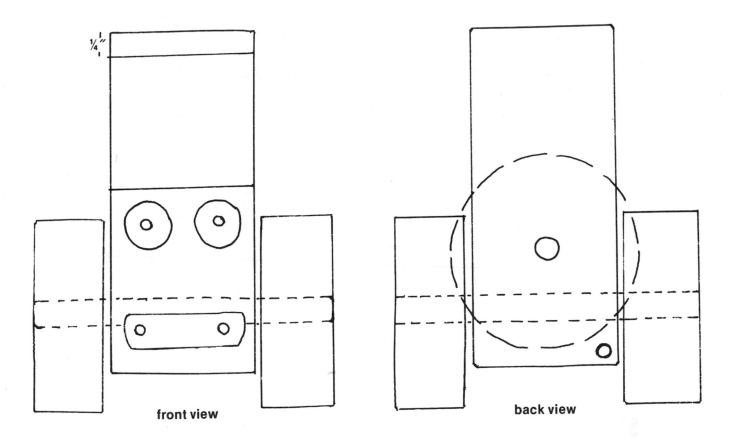

front view   **back view**

Cut out bumper from scrap piece and sand round and smooth.

Cut out window, starting with a ¼″ diameter drilled hole just within the window waste, threading the coping-saw blade into the hole and cutting out the window as usual. Open coping saw and remove blade when window is cut out.

Drill two ⅜″ diameter holes for axles as indicated.

Drill ¼″ diameter blind hole ½″ deep in back to attach spare tire as shown.

Drill one blind hole ³⁄₁₆″ diameter to a depth of ½″ below and to the right of spare hole, as marked, for tail pipe.

Drill two ³⁄₁₆″ diameter holes in bumper, use to mark through on wood with awl for matching holes, same diameter on car front.

Drill two ³⁄₁₆″ blind holes ¼″ deep, as marked, for bumper.

Sand lightly; being soft, redwood sands easily.

Cut five wheels ¾″ thick from 2″ diameter dowel, marking off the ¾″ as each is cut to insure accuracy.

Chamfer edges on four wheels only, sand fifth wheel smooth on one side. Sand wheels smooth.

Mark each wheel's exact center with an awl, located as shown.

In four wheels, drill ¼" diameter center hole for axles.

In fifth wheel, drill ¼" diameter blind hole ½" deep on the unsanded side of the wheel.

Cut two ⅜" thick sections of ½" diameter dowel for headlights. Sand one side of each smooth.

Glue headlights to body as marked, gluing rough side to front. Let dry.

Cut two 3¼" lengths of ¼" diameter dowel for axles.

Glue one axle end into one wheel flush with surface. Repeat with second axle and second wheel. Let dry.

Cut 1" length of ¼" diameter dowel, glue into spare wheel. Let dry.

Cut 1" length of ³⁄₁₆" diameter dowel for tail pipe.

Glue tail pipe into blind hole in back. Let dry.

Cut two ½" lengths of ³⁄₁₆" diameter dowel for bumper rivets.

Glue dowel lengths into bumper and then into blind holes. Let dry.

Glue spare and dowel into blind hole at back. Let dry.

Slip axle into front axle hole. Glue on third wheel, flush with wheel on outer side. Repeat for rear. Let dry.

Do final sanding; pay attention to glued axle ends, sanding all smooth without marks of excess glue.

Finish with part white shellac and part denatured alcohol to retain red hue, or use oil finish, renewing as needed. Unfinished, the wood fades somewhat to a weathered look, but unfinished toys do tend to get soiled as they are played with, and in most cases, dirt will have to be sanded off.

Jumping Bear

This jumping bear is a new interpretation of the jumping jack, a toy which was also called a polichinelle when it first came to colonial America with French settlers. It's a good crib toy, as it dances around when the string is pulled and the simple cord and wood construction make it safe as well. Just be sure to check occasionally for signs of teething, which sometimes causes wood to splinter. If so, you can refinish the edges and give the toy back to the child later on and it will seem like a new one again. To make a jumping bear, you'll need:

1 length of clear pine (or hardwood, which splinters much less) ½″ × 3½″ × 12″
1 small ball of braided cord or twine

Sand the length of wood smooth on both sides.
Trace the full-sized outlines of the bear.
Mark the pattern on the wood—one body, and four

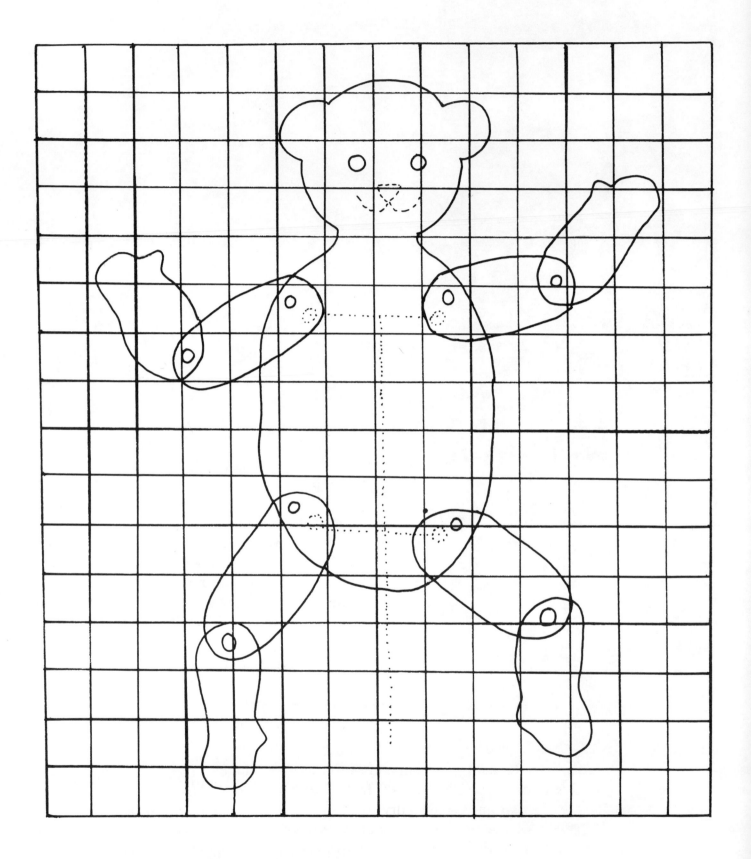

each of upper and lower arm and upper and lower leg parts, which are identical in shape.

Sand to smooth edges without rounding.

Drill ¼″ diameter holes, four in body to attach arms and legs, two for eyes, two each in upper-leg and upper-arm sections, and one each in lower-leg and lower-arm sections as indicated.

Drill one ¼″ diameter hole at upper edge of arms and legs as shown. Sand all drilled areas lightly if needed.

Cut one 18″ length of the cord. Make a tight knot in one end. Slip the other end through the hole in one lower-arm section. Pull lightly to see if the knot is large enough to hold, without slipping through the hole. If it slips, make another knot right next to it. It should work with one, however.

Take the end of the cord and slip it through the end of the upper arm which has only one hole in it. Tie a knot very close to the surface to secure, and cut the cord. Repeat for other arm and both legs, checking against the diagram to be sure that the parts fit together correctly for right and left sides.

Place the body facedown and position the arms and legs. Cut another length of cord and knot the arms and legs onto the body through the hole that is nearest to the center of the part. The holes near the edge are for the jumping mechanism. Use the same method of knotting on the sections as you did to tie them together.

Cut two 5″ lengths of cord. Knot one to the outermost hole in one arm and bring it to the matching hole in the opposite arm. Knot in place and trim off any extra cord. Repeat for legs as shown.

Cut one 12″ length of cord. Tie its end to the arm cord in its center, bring it down to the leg cord and knot once around it.

Let the end of the cord hang down, make two knots at the long end, and your bear's ready to jump. Try the action, pulling down on cord.

To secure the knots, you can add one drop of white liquid glue to each. Do all knots on front first and let dry. Then do the rear knots and let dry.

The bear can be finished with wax. If you prefer a gloss finish, paint the parts before you knot them in place.

Shaped-Outline Jigsaw Puzzle

Everyone likes jigsaw puzzles. A shaped-outline puzzle is all the more attactive as it becomes a sort of sculptural form which can lie flat or stand up when assembled.

This sleeping-cat puzzle is made out of 1″ pine. Until you are more familiar with the process, a softwood like pine is ideal, although hardwoods are very nice in this application. You'll need:

1 length of clear pine, 1″ × 5½″ × 10″

Sand each of the wide sides smooth, as the cutout parts are harder to sand with the grain.

Trace and enlarge outline for your pattern.

Transfer all of the lines onto the wood with carbon paper.

Practice cutting curves with your coping saw on a piece of scrap wood, changing the blade angle in the frame as needed. When using a fretsaw, the blade is fixed and the saw moves around due to its wider frame.

Cut out the shape.

Make the interior cuts for interlocking parts, starting with the one closest to the right edge.

Take each part off the body of the puzzle as it is cut to

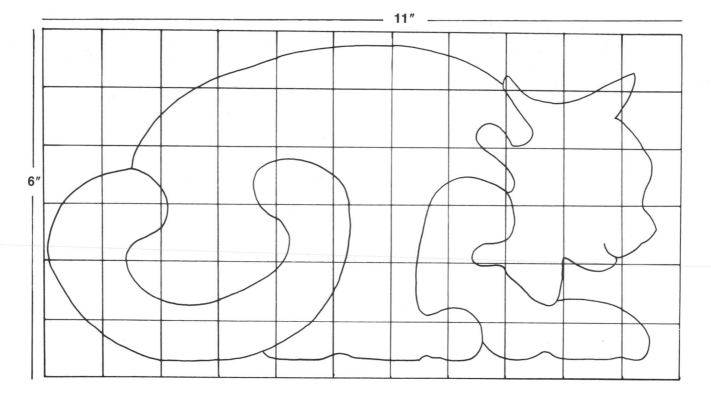

11″

6″

allow easier access to the next part, moving toward the left.

The last part is easiest to cut because you can move the saw more and change the blade angle less often. With a fretsaw, only the saw is moved throughout the cutting.

Sand the parts, removing any lines that marked the pattern and smoothing all sides without rounding corners.

Finish with one coat of part linseed oil and part turpentine, or clear wax.

You can make a shaped outline puzzle in any interesting shape that you choose, as long as it's not so wide or tall that the coping saw will have trouble reaching the interior cuts. A fretsaw is very good if you have one, since its frame allows you to cut farther into the wood.

If you enjoy painting simple objects or scenes, you can make a rectangular or square jigsaw puzzle. The painting can be done with oil paints on a smoothly sanded sheet of ½″ pine, as wide and as long as you like, since the smaller sections are cut off one at a time and your saw can easily reach all parts when you remove them as they are cut. Follow the diagrams for simple interior cuts you can make for a square or a rectangular puzzle. Finish all flat wood sides with oil or wax and use clear spray enamel to give one or two protective coats to the painted front.

Block Train

Trains are ever popular. You can make one with as many cars as you want since they are all based on the same principle. The difference is in their equipment and in how you shape the cars. The engine, boxcar, flatbed car, and caboose shown are all cut from a 3′ length of two by four. To make them, you'll need:

    1 length of pine, 1¾″ × 3¾″ × 36″
    1 dowel, ⅜″ diameter
    1 dowel, ½″ diameter
    2 dowels, ¼″ diameter
    2 dowels, 1″ and 1¾″ diameter, or
    16 wheels, 1″ diameter and 2 wheels, 1¾″ diameter

Trace pattern.
Transfer to wood.
Cut off each length with a crosscut saw and then shape with a coping saw.

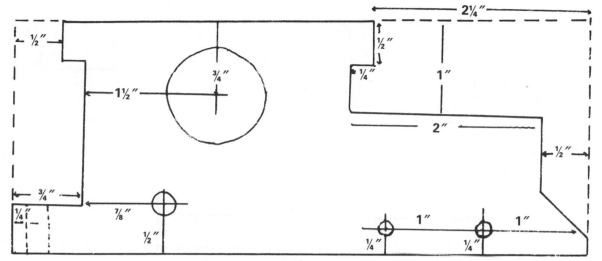

engine

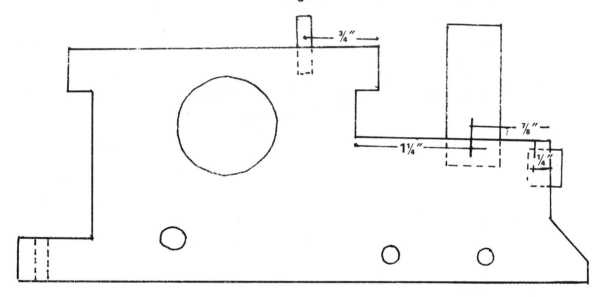

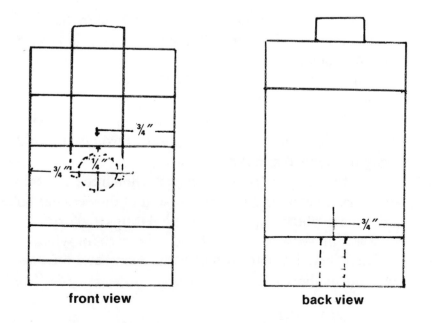

front view   **back view**

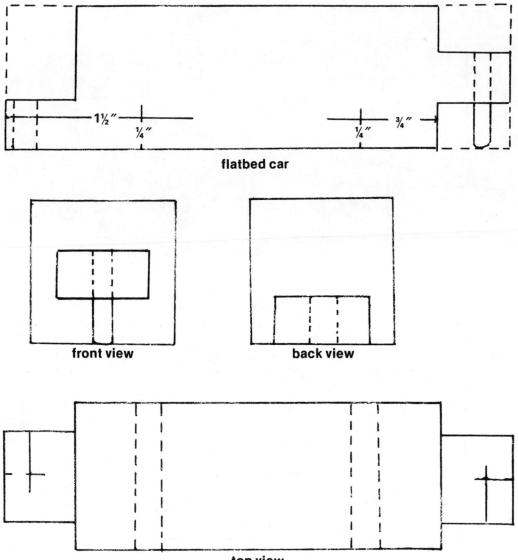

flatbed car

front view

back view

top view

Sand each car to shape and smooth, as shown.

Drill one ½″ diameter blind hole ½″ deep in engine for smokestack as shown.

Cut ½″ diameter dowel into 2″ length for smokestack. Glue in place. Let dry.

Drill ⁷⁄₁₆″ hole through front tab of boxcar, flatbed car, and caboose as shown. Drill ⅜″ hole through back tab of engine, boxcar, and flatbed car.

Cut three ¾″ lengths of ⅜″ dowel. Glue into back tabs of engine, boxcar, and flatbed car so that they extend below tabs as in photograph of uncoupled trains. Let dry.

Drill three ¾″ holes in caboose as shown for windows.

Drill two ⅜″ diameter holes in each car and three in engine as shown, for axles.

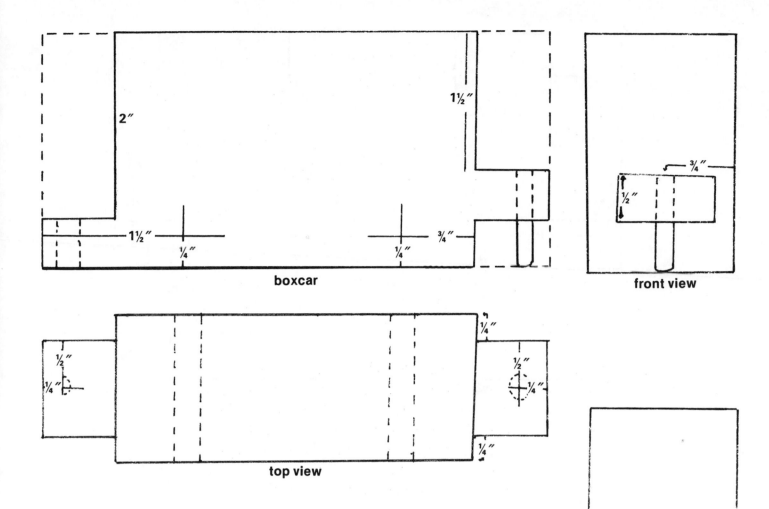

boxcar

front view

top view

back view

Cut nine 3″ lengths of ¼″ dowel for axle rods.

Cut sixteen ⅜″ thick wheels out of 1″ diameter dowel. Cut two ⅜″ thick wheels out of 1¾″ dowel. Sand to smooth. Drill one centered ¼″ diameter hole in each. Omit steps above if you're using wheels that you bought.

Glue one axle rod into one wheel, repeat eight times, for nine in all. Let dry.

Slip axles in place, position wheels following photograph, and glue in place. Let dry. Finish as desired after light sanding.

Test fit the ⅜″ dowel attachments in tabs. Trim as necessary so that dowel fits into front tab of following car without extending below lower tab when cars are coupled.

All you need now is the little engineer to drive the train.

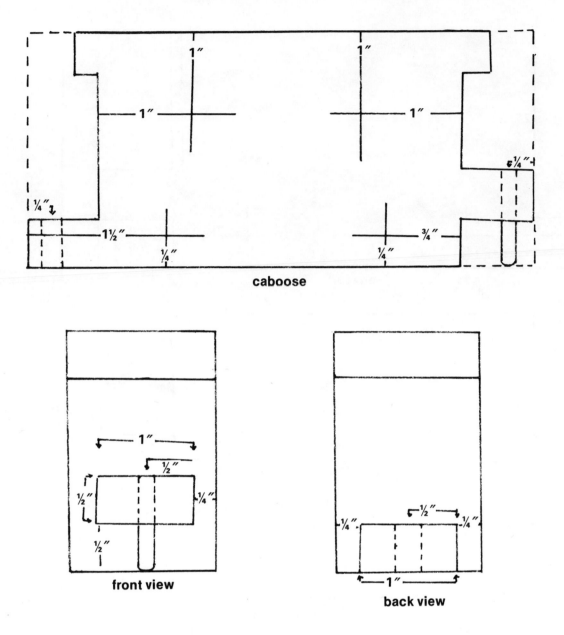

caboose

front view

back view

There are naturally many variations that you can make. The train can have just an engine and a caboose, or you can add more cars. It's up to you, as the basic design can be adapted to any type of train that you want to make.

Dowel Stacker

The dowel stacker can be a basic stacking toy which enables a young child to see the relationship of various sizes of the same shape, as you stack the concentrically sized discs on top of each other on their rod or arrange them into a male, female, or tree form. In nicely polished wood, it looks good in any sequence. You'll need:

1 length of pine, ¾″ × 4½″ × 18″
1 dowel, 2″ diameter
1 dowel, 1½″ diameter
1 dowel, 1″ diameter
1 wooden ball or bead, 1″ diameter (optional)
1 dowel, ¼″

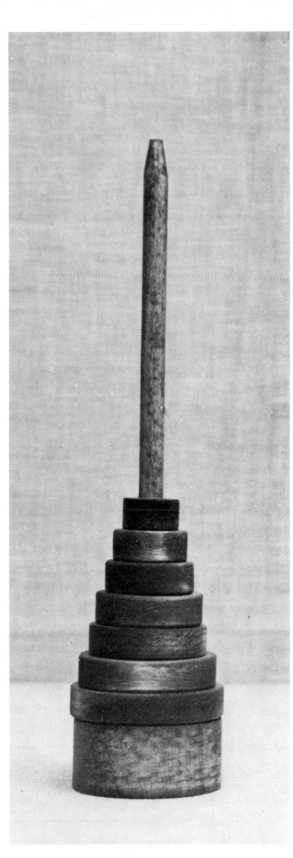

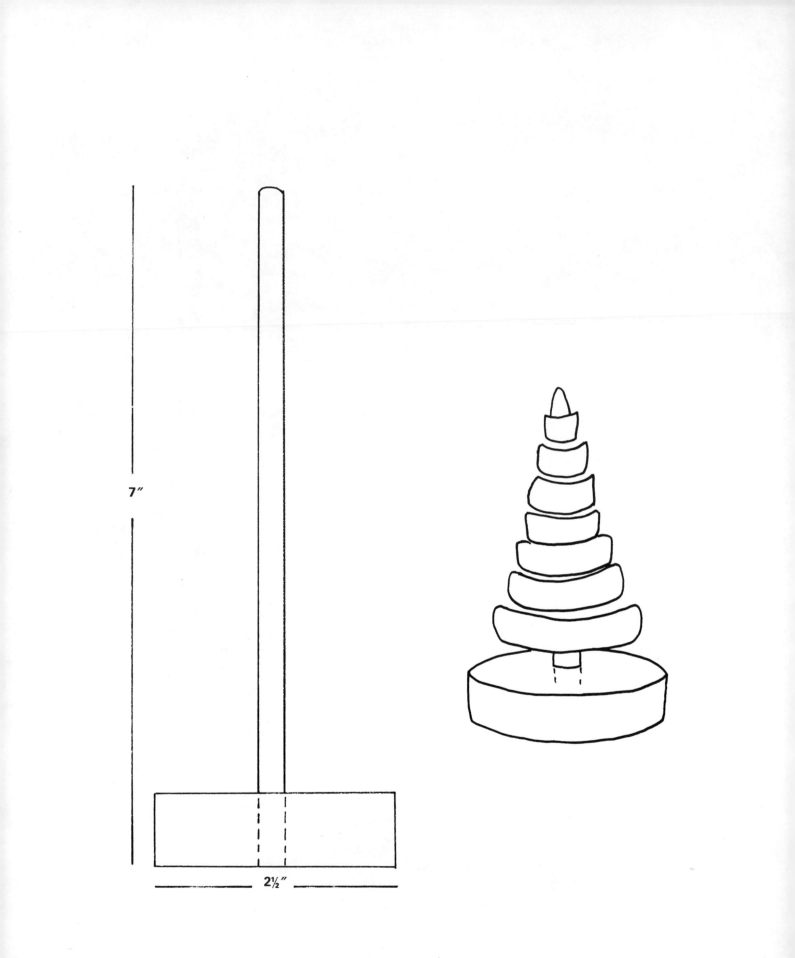

7″

2½″

Use a compass to draw circles on the wood, in sizes shown, of 4½″, 4″, 3½″, 3″, 2½″ in diameter.

Cut out the circles and sand edges slightly round and smooth.

Mark the 4½″ circle at the exact center and drill a hole that is ¼″ diameter.

Cut a 6½″ length of the ¼″ diameter dowel. (For bead, cut 7″.)

Glue the dowel into the 4½″ circle, flush with one side. Let dry.

Cut ¾″ sections of the 2″, 1½″, and 1″ diameter dowels and sand edges slightly round and smooth.

Mark each of the circles with exact center hole.

Drill center holes ⅜″ in diameter.

Drill ⅜″ diameter blind hole in ball ½″ deep. Bead requires no drilling, as 1″ diameter wooden beads are usually drilled with ¼″ holes. This will make a tight fit on the slightly longer dowel used with a bead, since the hole goes all the way through and the drilled top knob goes in only ½″. If the hole is too small, expand to ⅜″, using the existing small hole as a starter for the drilling.

See diagram and photograph for three-dowel base.

Finish all sections with shellac, varnish, or other shiny finish. String on a thin rope for painting and drying.

When they are finished, the dowel sections and pine sections will take the finishing agent differently, so that you'll have a variety of wood tones in the complete dowel stacker.

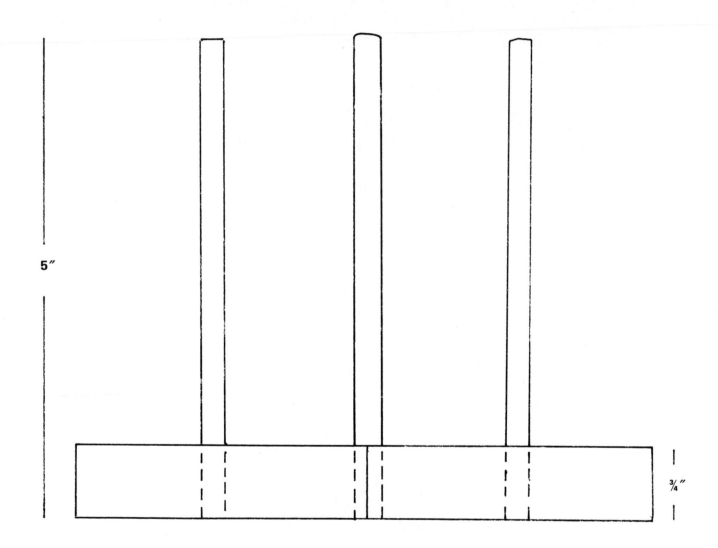

5″

¾″

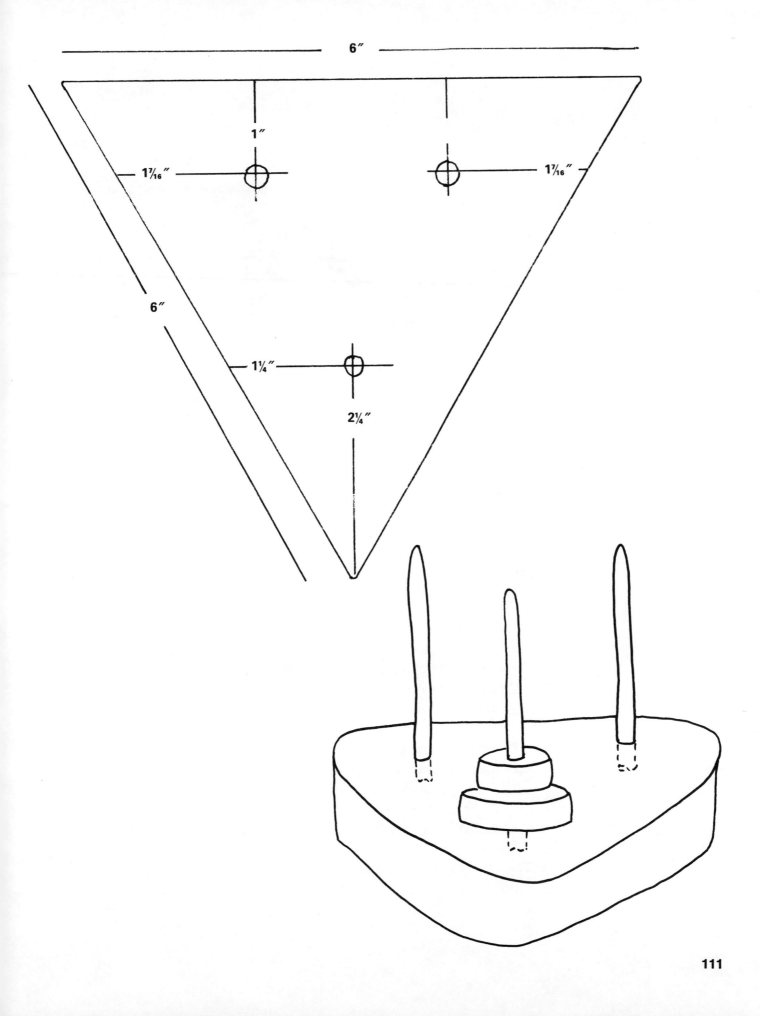

Stick Horse

The horse's head on a stick is one of the oldest types of toy, a friend to imaginative children through the ages. This version has wheels, but if you like to simplify things, the end of the stick can be rounded off and left as is, without a wheel assembly at all. To make the model shown, you'll need:

1 length of pine, $1\frac{1}{2}'' \times 7\frac{1}{2}'' \times 12''$
1 dowel, 3' long, $\frac{3}{4}''$ diameter
2 wheels, $\frac{3}{4}''$ thick, 2" diameter, with $\frac{1}{2}''$ center holes
1 dowel, $\frac{1}{2}''$ diameter
1 length of pine, $1\frac{3}{4}'' \times 1\frac{3}{4}'' \times 4''$ for wheel assembly.

(The last three items can be omitted if you're making a plain-end stick.)

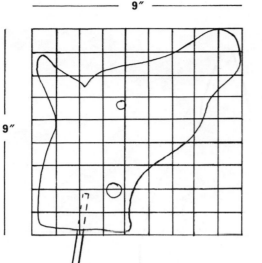

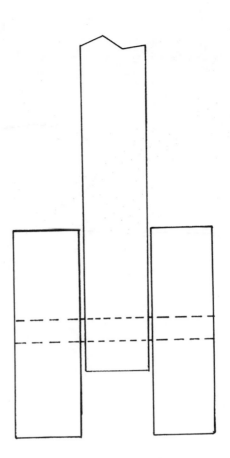

Trace and enlarge the horse's head pattern.

Sand the length of wood for the head smooth on both sides.

Transfer the outlines onto the smooth wood.

Cut out the shape with a coping saw.

Sand smooth, including edges, without rounding.

Cut the ¾″ thick dowel into two parts, one 6″ and the other the remaining length, which can be cut down, if desired, for a young child.

Round the ends of the 6″ length of dowel. If you're omitting wheels, round off the long section at one end only.

Drill ¾″ diameter blind hole ¾″ deep in base of head as shown.

Drill ¾″ hole for handle as marked.

Sand lightly.

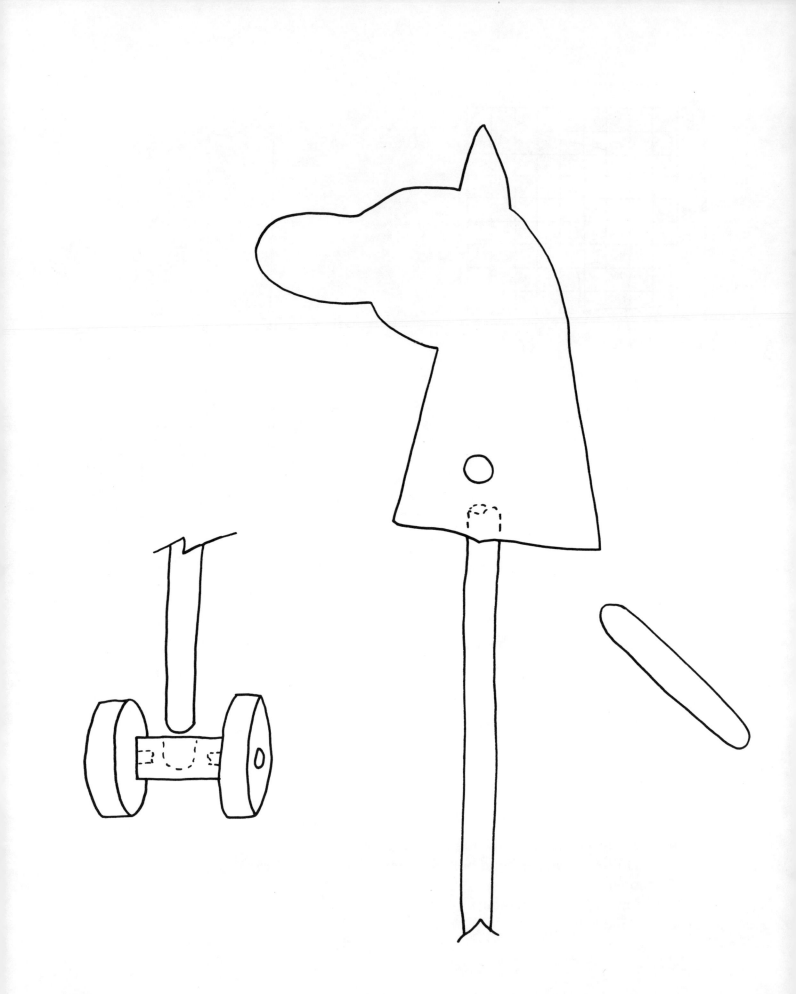

Slip 6″ dowel into hole, sanding dowel, if needed, to fit.

Glue in place, with an equal length of dowel extending out beyond head on either side to create handles. Let dry.

Glue end of stick into base of head, sanding stick, if needed, to fit. Let dry.

If you're not using wheels, glue in unfinished end of stick and skip to finishing, as rest of steps are for wheel assembly.

Drill ¾″ diameter blind hole ⅝″ deep in one 4″ side of block as shown.

Drill ⅝″ diameter hole through block from 1¾″ side as marked.

Glue one wheel to end of ½″ diameter dowel. Let dry.

Slide into block, fit on second wheel, and then cut the dowel to suit. Glue the wheel in place. Let dry.

Glue stick dowel into the blind hole in block. Let dry.

For a natural finish, use one or two coats of shellac and alcohol, or other clear finish.

If you like, the horse can be painted with a face and fitted with leather reins and a leather mane.

All you need is the rider, and the stick horse can gallop indefinitely.

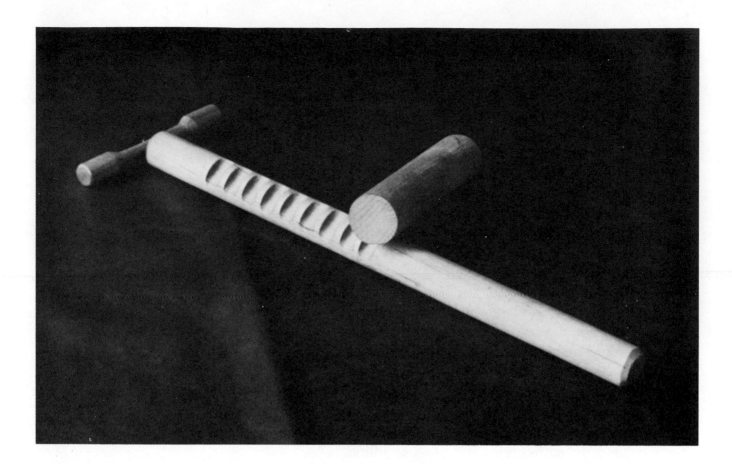

Whimmy Diddle

A whimmy diddle is a colonial toy that is interesting to all as they try to figure out the secret—which you already know—of how to make its propeller spin in one direction or the other on command. It's a carefully notched large dowel rod, originally made with a hardwood narrow branch, with a propeller at the end and a shorter dowel rod that you rub on the notches as you hold the whimmy diddle parallel to the ground.

You hold the short rod in your right hand and the long rod in your left hand, and rub the notches on the long rod with the short rod. If you place your left thumb against the right side of the long rod, the propeller spins to the right, or clockwise. If you place your left forefinger alongside of the notches on the left side of the long rod, the propeller spins to the left, or counterclockwise. That's the trick, but only the most observant will notice just what you're doing if you don't tell. To make a whimmy diddle, you'll need:

1 dowel, 9¾″ in length, ¾″ diameter
1 dowel, 4¾″ in length, ⅝″ diameter
1 dowel, 3½″ in length, ⅝16″ diameter
1 flathead nail, head of 3⁄16″ diameter

Sand the dowels, rounding off cut edges.

Shape the shortest dowel for the propeller as shown.

Mark the largest dowel rod for notches. They are placed as shown, precisely ¼″ wide, with a wood separation of ⅛″ between each one.

Cut out the notches with a coping saw, or file in with a file.

Drill a 1⁄16″ hole in the propeller, centering it exactly as indicated.

Test the propeller on the nail to see that it spins freely; if not, drill a 3⁄32″ hole.

When the hole is right, leave the nail in the propeller.

Mark the center of one end of the large dowel with an awl.

Drill a very short 1⁄16″ pilot hole and nail on the propeller, leaving room between the nailhead and dowel of at least 3⁄16″.

One light coat of linseed oil is a fine finish on the closely grained hardwood that dowels are made out of, and your whimmy diddle is complete.

4¾″

9¾″

3½″

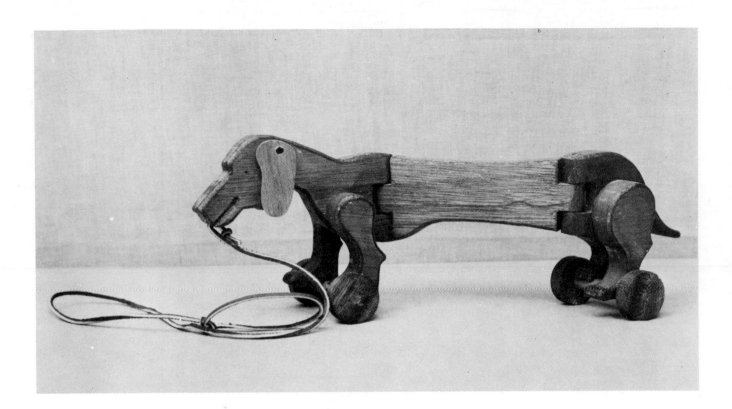

Dachshund

This bendable dachshund is made out of mahogany to represent the color of the dog after which it is patterned. You can have equally good results using pine if you prefer, as mahogany is both harder to work with and more expensive. The hinged body bends as the dog is pulled and its doweled ears flop. To make it, you'll need:

1 length of 3′ wood (any type), 1″ × 5½″
1 dowel, ¼″ diameter
4 wheels, 2″ diameter × ¾″ thick
1 length of narrow rawhide, about 2′ long

Sand the flat surfaces of the wood.
Trace all pattern parts.
Mark on wood using carbon paper (a light color for the darker woods).

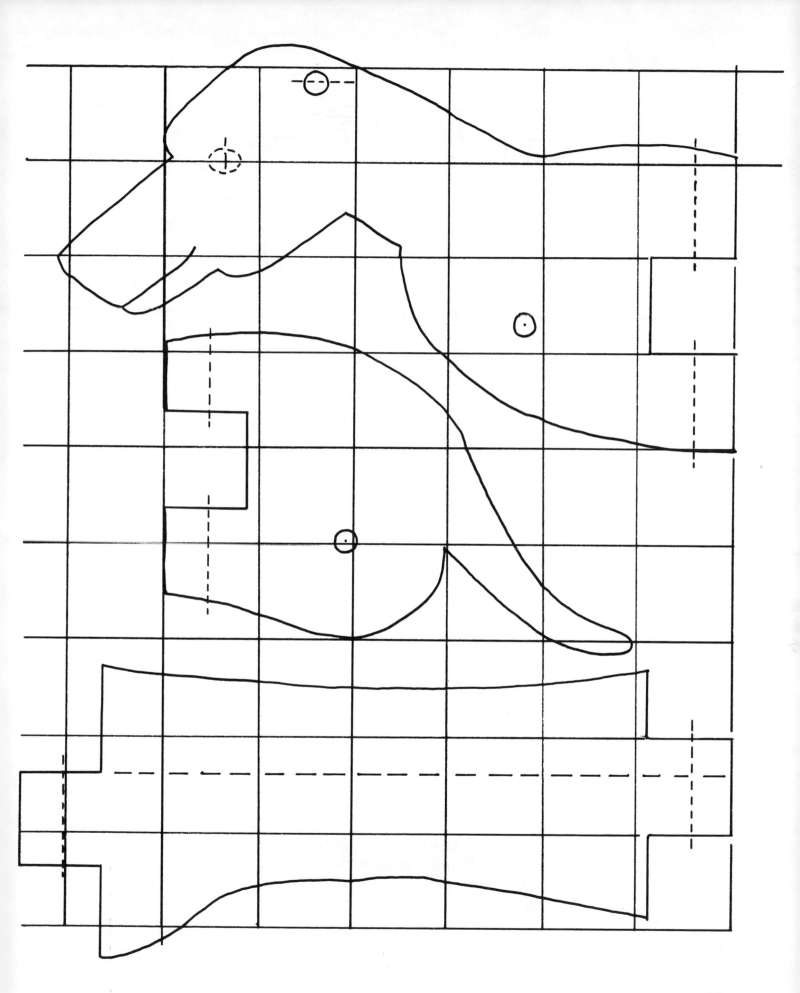

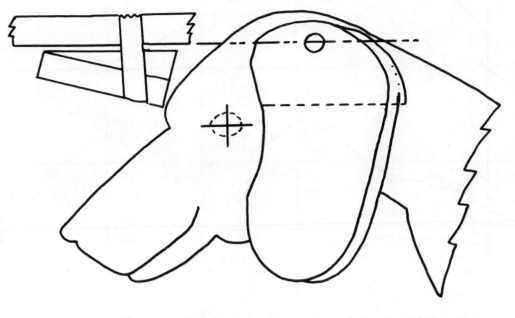

Cut out the three body parts and the four legs. Cut out one ear section and one ear wedge section, both of which will be split later on.

Drill ⅜" diameter holes in the body parts as shown to make the swivel joints, and ¼" diameter holes for upper and lower parts to complete the joint holes.

Drill one ⅜" diameter hole through head for ears as marked.

Drill ¼" deep, ¼" diameter blind holes in body and inner-leg sections as shown. Sand parts smooth as needed.

For a standard wheel and axle, as used in the cars, drill ⅜" diameter holes at leg bottoms.

Sand down the edges of joints to allow them to bend and turn. Fit together to check.

When you are satisfied with the movement of the modified mortise and tenon joint, slip in the ¼" dowel, sanding, if needed, to fit into top and bottom holes which are smaller than the central one, which needs the room to swivel.

Mark the dowel for the exact lengths of the two joints and cut. Fit back in place as shown and glue. Let dry.

Cut four ⅜" long sections of dowel and use to plug the legs to body with glue as shown. Let dry.

Cut ear section in half widthwise to make two ears. Glue each to the proper side of the wedge as shown. Clamp well and dry.

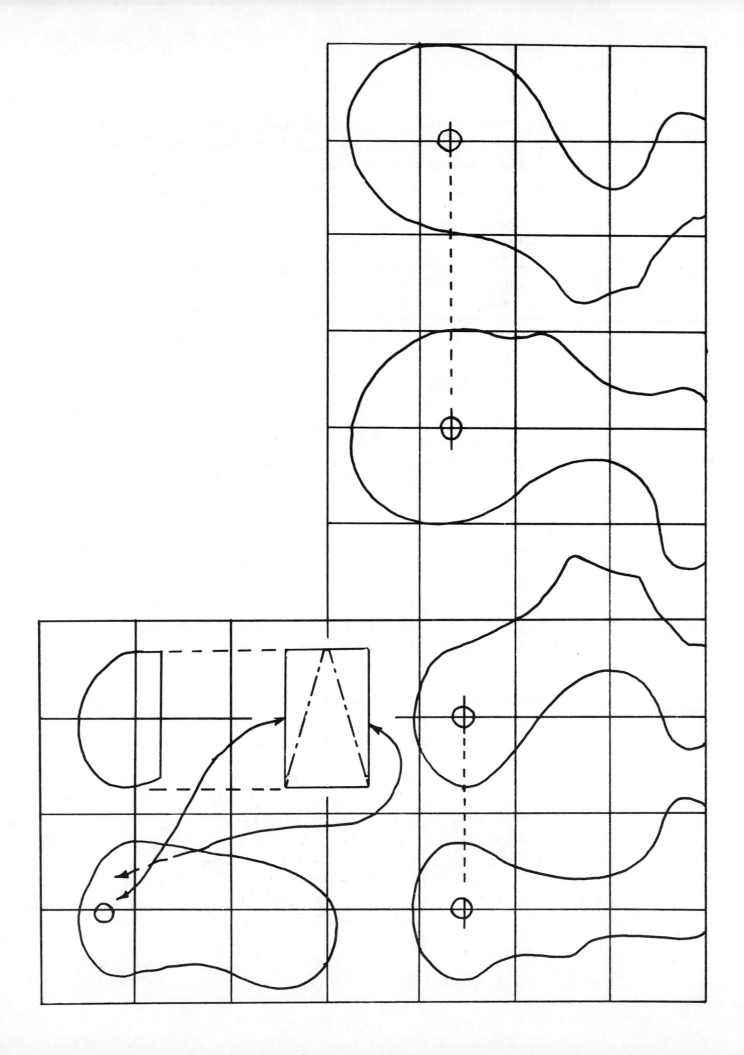

Slice off the ears through the wedge, forming two angled sections as indicated. These allow the ears to stand out at an angle from the head.

Drill one ¼" diameter hole into each ear as shown.

Cut a 1⅞" length of ¼" diameter dowel and glue into one ear hole with the dowel slightly recessed as shown. Let dry.

Slip ear rod through ear hole, position second ear so that it is parallel to the first, and glue in place. Let dry.

Glue two ¼" diameter dowel lengths of 4¾" each into one wheel each. Let dry.

Slip axles into axle holes in legs, position the other two wheels, and let dry.

Sand lightly.

Finish with linseed oil.

To pull the dog, you can tie the rawhide leash around its neck or make a special hole in the mouth and glue the rawhide in place. To do this, drill a blind hole, ¼" diameter, ½" deep, directly into the mouth. Glue one end of the rawhide into the hole carefully to avoid dripping any glue and let dry completely.

Hinged shapes, based on the mortise and tenon type of joint, are fascinating. You can make many different animal shapes that will look great as they bend and turn. Once you see how well these jointed shapes work, you'll want to create all sorts of swiveling forms on wheels.

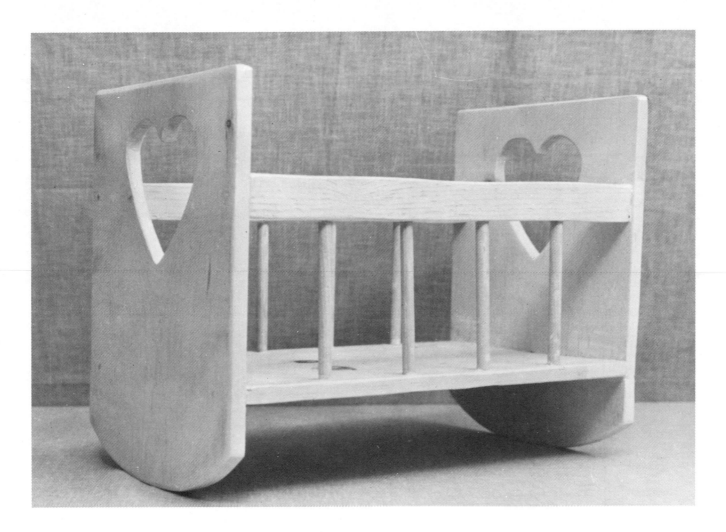

Incised Heart Cradle

You can make a cradle with pine and dowels, which will be appreciated by all those children who love to play with dolls and stuffed animals. To make the one shown, you'll need:

2 lengths of pine, ½″ × 9¼″ × 12″
1 length of pine, ½″ × 9″ × 14″
2 lengths of pine, ½″ × 1½″ × 14″
8 dowels, ¼″ diameter, 5″ long
1 dowel, ⅛″ diameter

Sand down the width of each plank.
Copy head- and footboard pattern parts and transfer to wood.

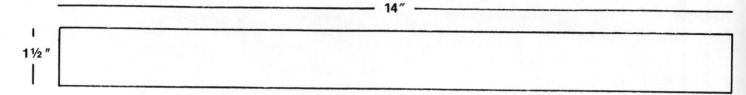

side rail plank

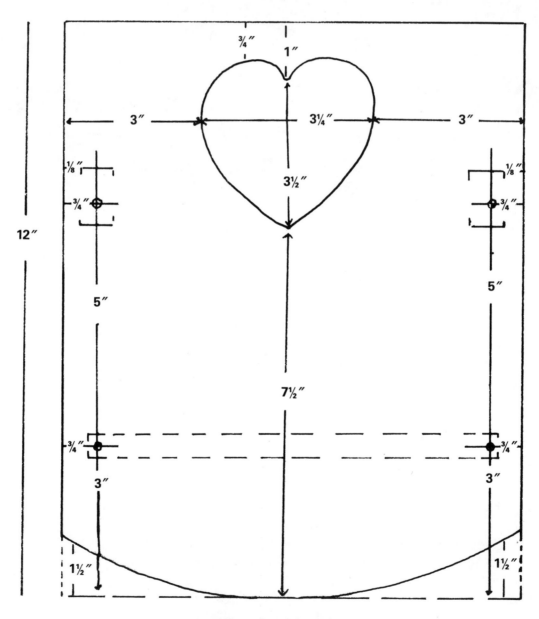

headboard and footboard

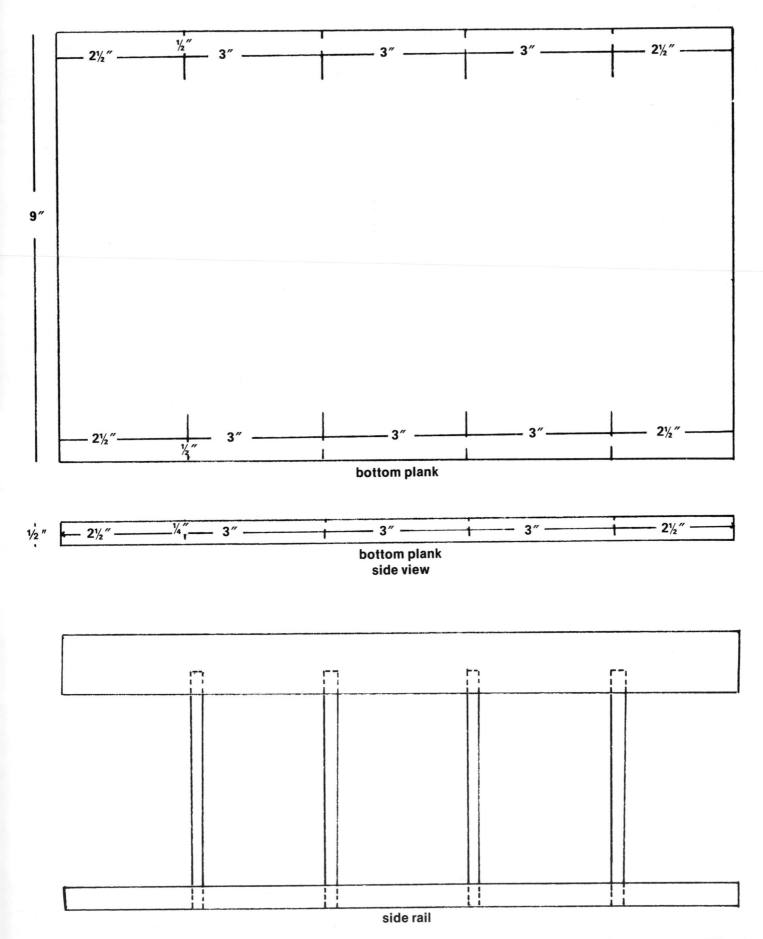

bottom plank

**bottom plank
side view**

side rail

Cut lengths, if required, with crosscut saw.

Cut out pattern shape with coping saw.

Sand cuts smooth without rounding edges.

Cut out incised heart in headboard and footboard. Use drill to make hole within the waste, and coping saw threaded into the hole to cut out the heart shape. Repeat for second piece. Sand interior cut smooth and slightly round.

Mark lines for 1 × 2 lengths of pine for sides.

Cut dowel following diagram, drill on bottom and matching holes in side rails for dowel bars as shown.

Glue dowel pieces into sides, then into bottom. Let dry. Glue to assemble rest as shown.

Cut four ⅝″ lengths of ⅛″ dowel and use as pegs to secure joints in place in headboard and footboard. Let dry.

Sand lightly, as needed, to smooth edges, particularly on bottom.

Finish as desired. Any natural finish is attractive.

You may want to paint the cradle with bright enamel or perhaps with simple folk art motifs to match the heart shape or complement it with stylized flowers.

Pattern variations can be achieved by changing the dimensions of the cradle to suit different purposes. This is easy to do with the square grid enlargement, as you can reduce it, to miniature size for a doll house, to 7″ long instead of 14″ for small dolls or to 21″ long for large-sized dolls and stuffed animals.

Rocking Horse

A rocking horse is a large toy that is not as difficult to make as you might expect. The horse can be finished to retain its natural wood grain, or painted for an entirely different look. To make one, you'll need:

1 length of pine, ¾″ × 8½″ × 10′, for two body parts and tail
1 length of pine, ½″ × 3¾″ × 6′, for legs
1 length of pine, 1¾″ × 3¾″ × 6′, for rockers
1 length of pine, ¾″ × 11¼″ × 5′, for head
1 length of pine, 1″ × 7½″ × 12″, for saddle
1 dowel, ¼″ diameter, for plug joints
1 length of leather stripping, 5′ long and 1″ wide, for reins.

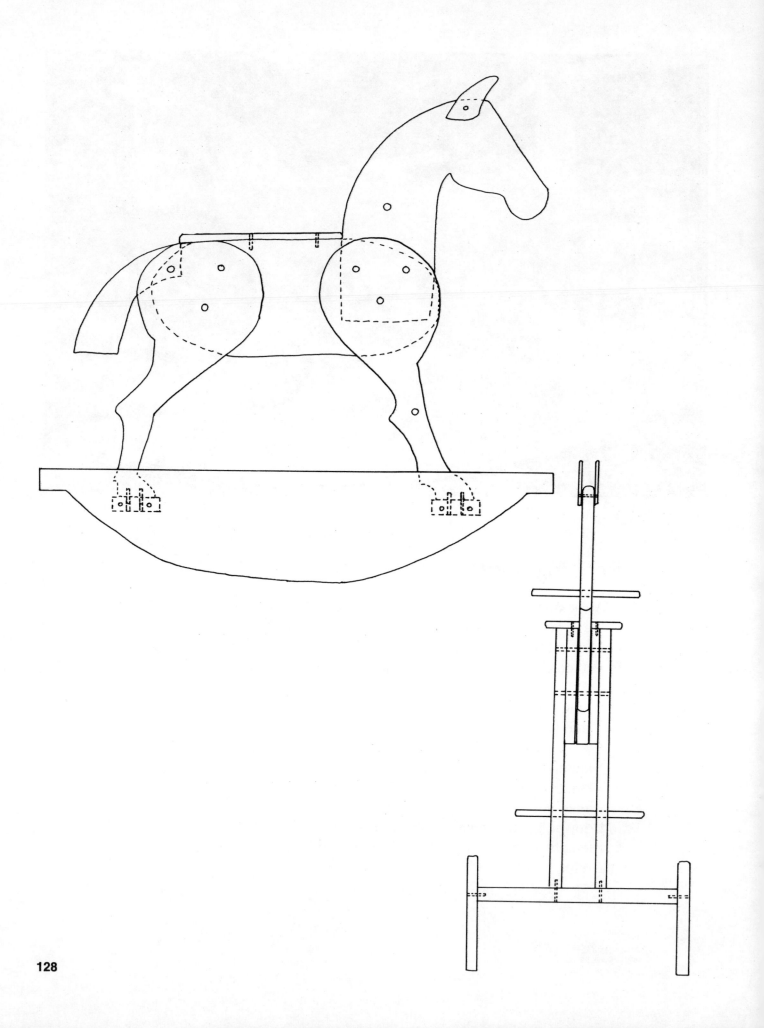

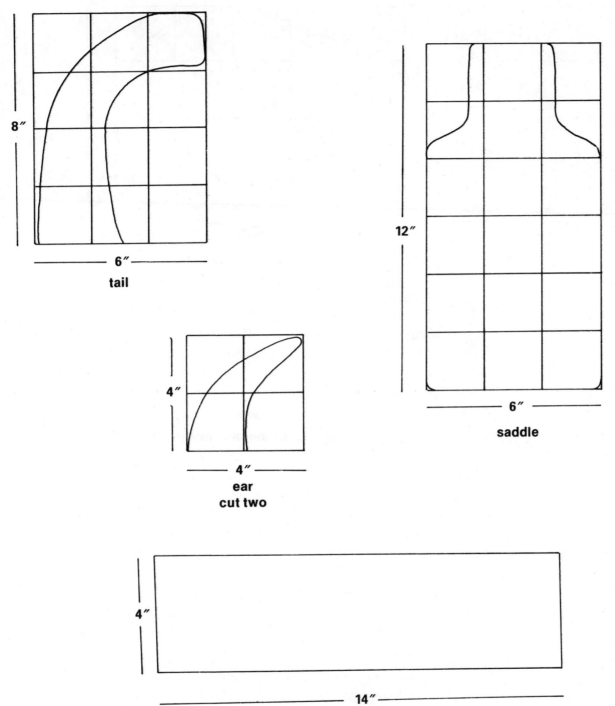

8″

6″

tail

4″

4″

ear
cut two

12″

6″

saddle

4″

14″

crossbar
cut two

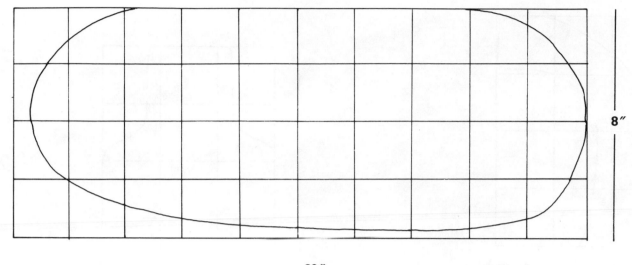

8″

20″
body
cut two

Sand down both sides of the wood to smooth.

Trace and enlarge pattern for head, body, and tail parts.

Mark on sanded wood.

Use crosscut saw to cut away excess wood, allowing coping saw to get close enough to the outlines to cut them out. Or, if you have access to a saber saw, use it to cut out the outline.

Make leg pattern, transfer to wood and cut out.

Make rocker pattern, transfer and cut out.

Make saddle pattern, transfer and cut out.

Make ear pattern and transfer onto leftover wood from head. Cut out.

Sand all edges smooth.

Glue lower neck, on head part, in between two body parts as shown. Drill ¼″ holes through the three layers of neck and body and glue in strengthening 2¼″ dowel pegs.

Attach ears to head by gluing 2¼″ long dowel peg into ¼″ diameter hole through head and ears. Let dry.

Glue tail in between two back ends of body parts. Secure by gluing 2¼″ dowel into ¼″ hole drilled through three layers of body and tail.

Glue legs in place as indicated. Strengthen with dowel pegs, cut to fit into blind holes drilled through legs partway into body. Let dry.

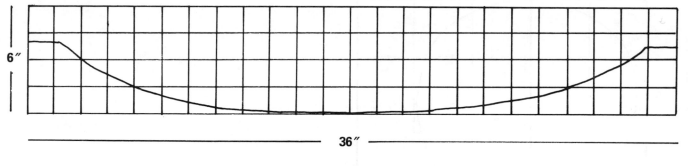

6″

36″

rocker
cut two

16″

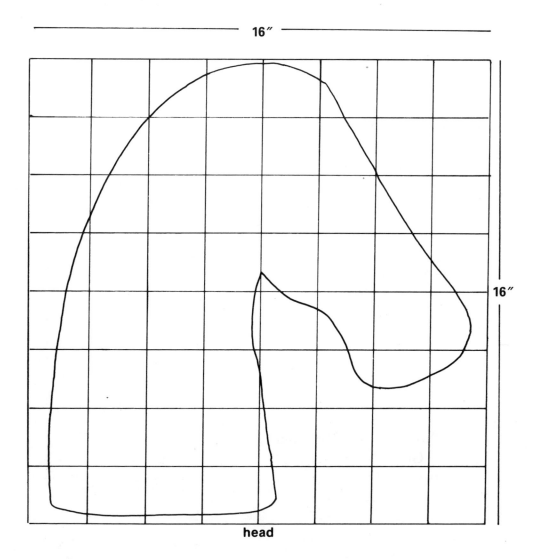

16″

head

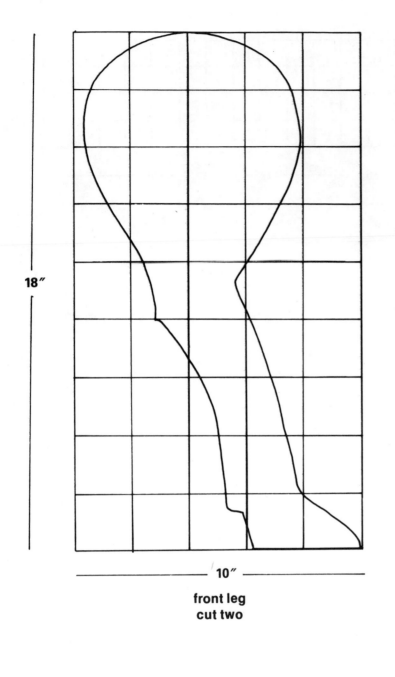

18″

10″

**front leg
cut two**

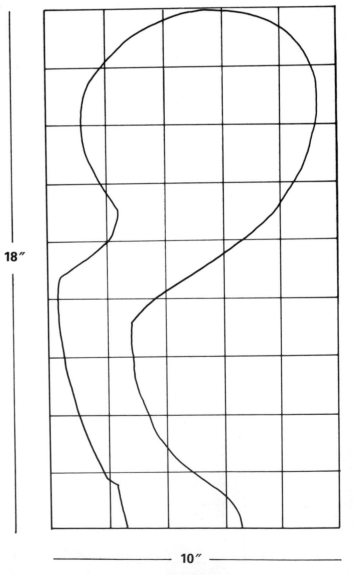

18″

10″

**back leg
cut two**

Cut two crossbars for rockers from excess wood from body's plank. Attach to inside of rockers through blind hole with dowel pegs as shown. Let dry.

Attach saddle to body with dowel pegs and glue as shown. Let dry.

Drill ¼″ diameter holes in hoofs and matching blind holes into tops of crossbars as shown.

Attach legs through holes, using dowel pegs cut to size shown. Let dry.

Sand all for final sanding.

Finish as desired.

Loop reins around neck, knot once, and bring ends back to saddle.

For a foot support, have the child try the rocking horse and mark appropriate level on leg, at foot height. Cut a 6–8″ length of ½″ diameter dowel. Drill ½″ diameter hole at mark; insert dowel and glue in place.

Cricket

This hopping cricket was made out of a two and a half foot piece of walnut, which was discovered on a forgotten pile of cut wood odds and ends in the cutting room of a local lumberyard. Its deep color and closely textured grain are outstanding. As a hardwood, it is definitely so when it comes to cutting it out. If you prefer easier cutting, use clear pine in the same dimensions. You'll need:

1 length of walnut, ⅞″ × 3½″ × 28″
1 dowel, ½″ diameter
1 dowel, ⅜″ diameter
1 dowel, ¼″ diameter
1 dowel, ⅛″ diameter
2 wheels, ⅝″ thick, 2″ diameter
2 wheels, ⅞″ thick, 1⅝″ diameter
1 wooden ball or round bead, 1¾″ diameter

Trace and enlarge pattern for body, front legs, upper and lower back legs.

Sand wood smooth.

Transfer pattern with light carbon paper for walnut, or regular for pine.

Cut out all parts with a coping saw. Go slowly but steadily and pause if the blade starts to heat up.

Drill ⅜″ diameter holes as marked, for eye, mid-body hole, and rear axle. Drill two ⅛″ diameter blind holes in top front of head as shown.

Sand body and each part as you complete the holes. Soften edges.

Cut one ⅞″ length of ⅜″ diameter dowel. Glue into eye. Let dry.

Cut two ½″ lengths of ⅛″ diameter dowel. Glue into blind holes at front top of head for antennae. Let dry.

Into each 2″ diameter back wheel, drill one ¼″ diameter blind hole ½″ deep, ⅝″ from center on radius as shown.

Cut two 1¼″ lengths of ¼″ diameter dowel, glue one into each wheel in blind hole to make one peg in each wheel. Let dry.

Drill ¼″ diameter hole at wide end of upper (back) leg as shown. Repeat. Drill ⁷⁄₁₆″ diameter hole in narrow end of upper leg; repeat for second upper leg. Sand both smooth.

Drill ¼″ diameter hole at wide end of lower leg; repeat for second lower leg. Drill ⁷⁄₁₆″ diameter hole at narrow end of lower leg as indicated; repeat for second lower leg. Sand smooth.

Glue one upper leg's ¼″ hole to one 2⅜″ length of ¼″ diameter dowel. Let dry.

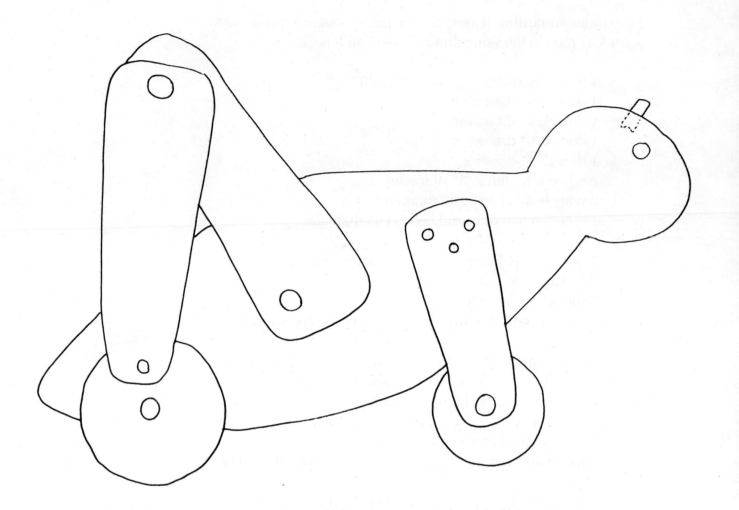

Glue one lower leg section's ¼″ hole to one 4½″ length of ¼″ diameter dowel. Let dry.

Drill one ½″ diameter axle hole in each front leg as shown.

Glue front legs to body as shown. Let dry.

Drill three dowel peg holes, each ⅛″ in diameter, through front legs, as marked, to a depth of 1⅜″.

Cut six 1¼″ lengths of ⅛″ dowel, glue and insert into holes in front legs. Let dry.

Cut one 4⅜″ length of ½″ dowel front axle.

Glue front axle to one wheel of 1⅝″ diameter, enlarging wheel hole if needed to fit. Let dry.

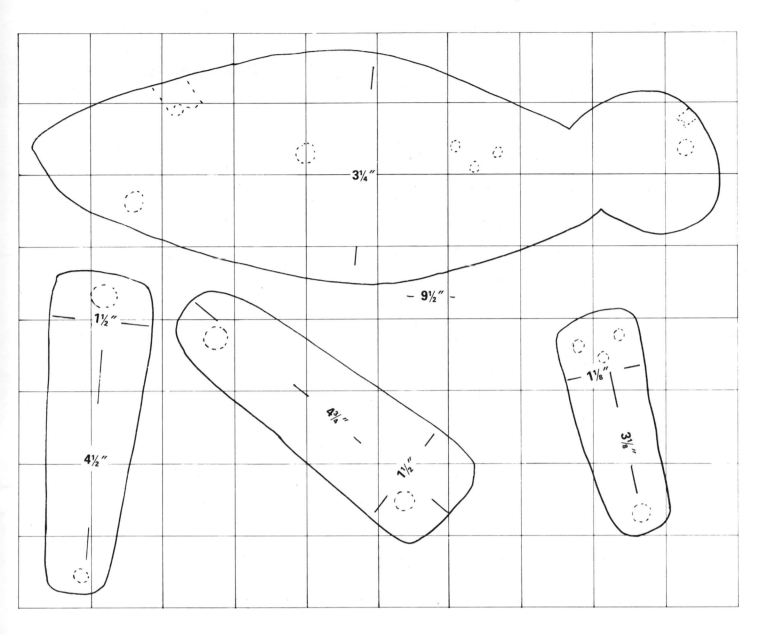

Glue one back wheel to a 2⅜″ length of ¼″ diameter dowel with short length of dowel on wheel heading away from axle. Let dry.

Slip in front axle. Glue second 1⅝″ wheel. Let dry.

Slip in back axle. Glue second 2″ wheel on axle. Make sure that the dowel peg in the outer wheel is facing out, away from the axle, and that the pegs on both wheels are in the same position. Let dry.

Slip rod, attached to wide end of upper back leg, into hole in mid-body. Match up second upper leg on other side, glue onto dowel. Let dry.

Slip the dowel attached to the wide end of the lower leg

through both $\frac{7}{16}$″ holes of upper leg. Position narrow end of lower leg on peg in wheel.

Place second lower leg on dowel leading from the first one and on the peg in the second back wheel; glue to dowel only, not peg. Let dry.

Push forward to see the cricket hop.

Drill one $\frac{1}{2}$″ diameter blind hole $\frac{5}{8}$″ deep into width of body, between rear wheels, as shown. Drill same size in ball.

Cut one 13″ length of $\frac{1}{2}$″ diameter dowel. Glue ball to end. Let dry. For bead, enlarge hole if needed and make the dowel 13½″ in length. Glue as for wheel, flush with dowel. Let dry.

Glue plain end of dowel into body of cricket. Let dry.

Finish with part white shellac and part denatured alcohol. Use two coats, letting the first dry completely, sanding lightly, and applying the second.

Noah's Ark

Noah's ark has a removable, dowel-pegged roof that fits into the cabin. The floor of the cabin is fitted with ½″ strips, which hold the animals in place. It is best to assemble the ark with all parts precut. You'll need:

For Hull (all wood is clear pine and hardwood dowels):
    2 sides, ½″ × 3¼″ × 10″
    4 front and rear blocks, 1⅛″ × 2¾″ × 4½″
    1 bottom, ½″ × 4½″ × 10¼″

12 dowel pegs, ⅛" diameter, each 1" long

4 dowel pegs, ⅛" diameter, each 1½" long

For Cabin:

2 sides, ½" × 4½" × 8"

2 front and back, ½" × 3½" × 4½"

4 strips, ½" × ½", each 6½" long

For Roof:

1 length of wood, ¼" × 3¼" × 8¾"

1 length of wood, ¼" × 3" × 8¾"

1 length of wood, ½" × 3¼" × 4½", cut into two roof blocks as shown

4 dowel pegs, ⅜" diameter, each ¾" long

8 dowel pegs, ⅛" diameter, each ½" long

For Animals:

1 length of wood ½" × 6" × 2' (or any ½" stock that is wide enough to draw pattern parts)

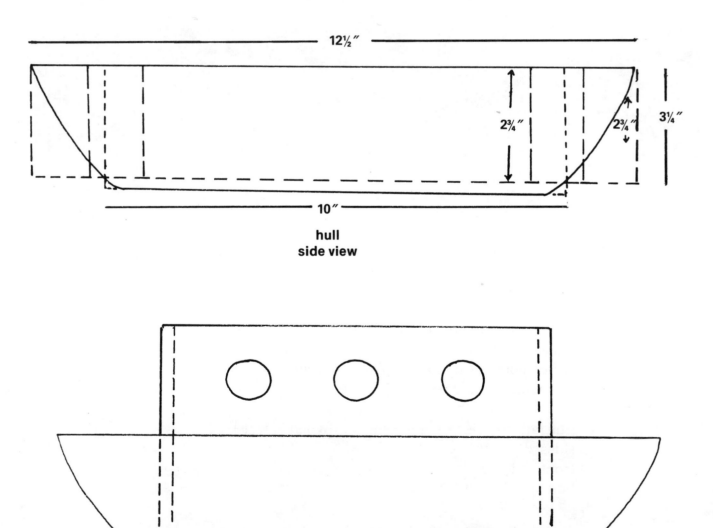

hull
side view

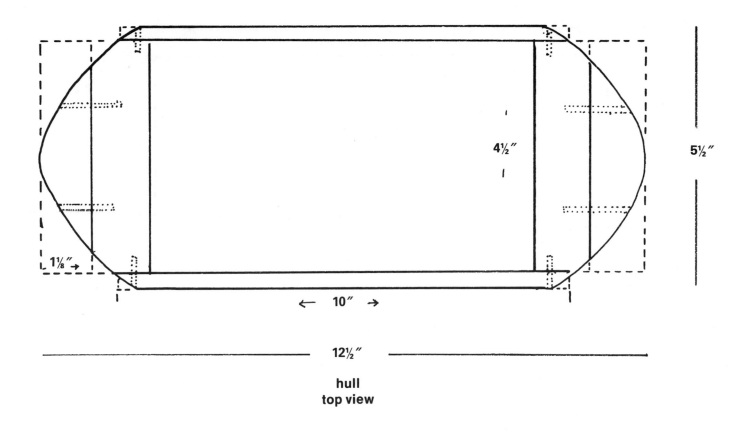

5½″

4½″

1⅛″ →

← 10″ →

12½″

**hull
top view**

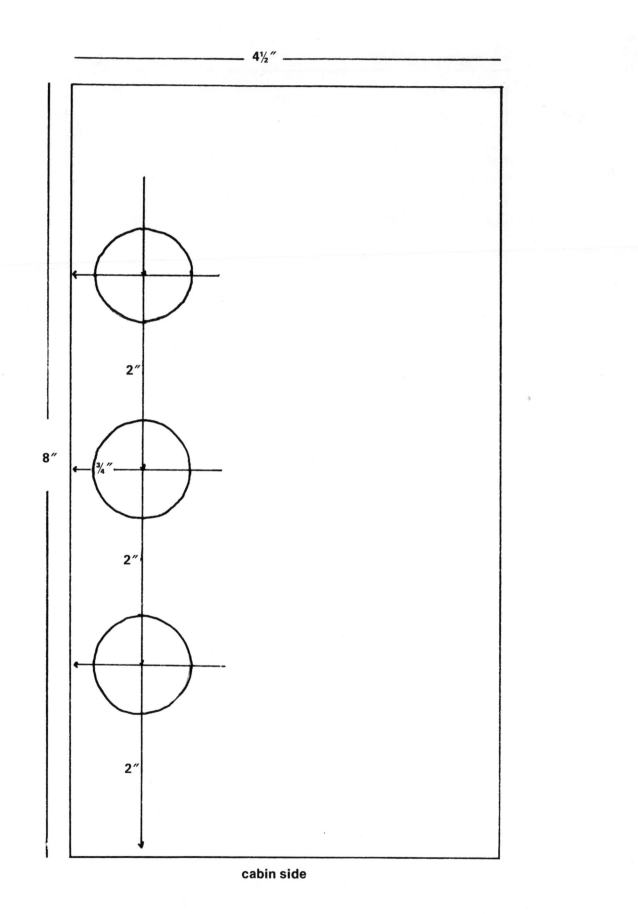

cabin side

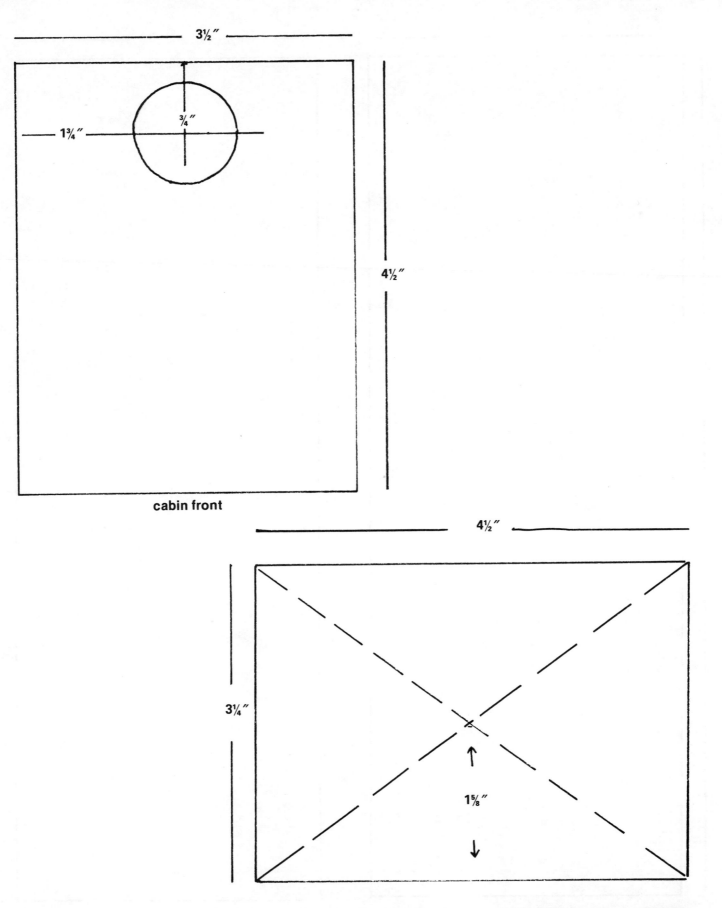

3½″

1¾″

¾″

4½″

cabin front

4½″

3¼″

1⅝″

cutting diagram for roof block

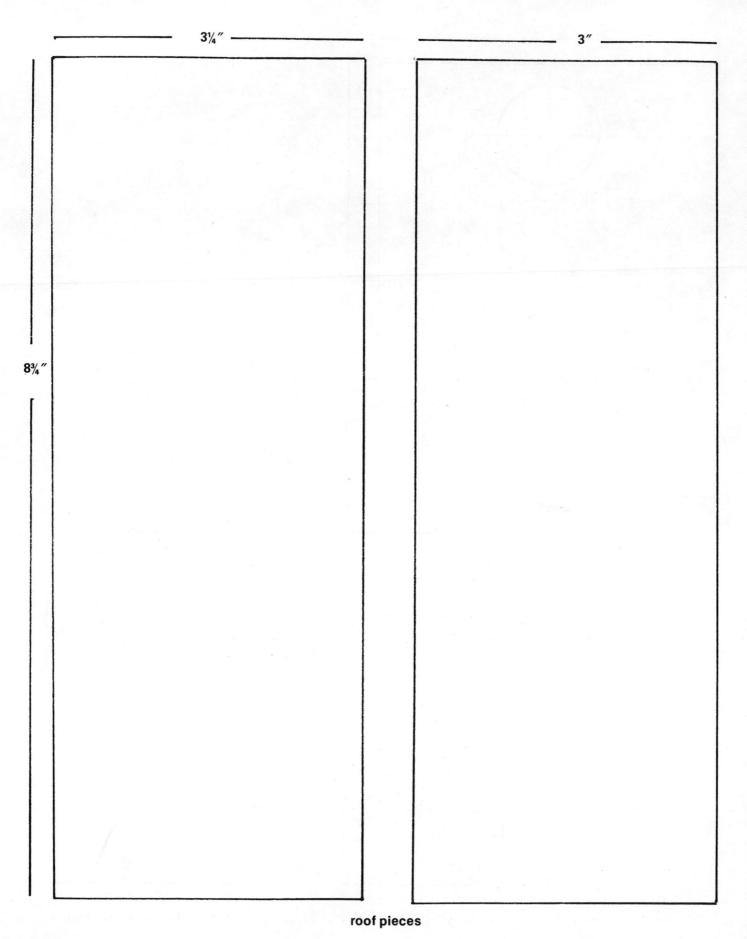

3¼″

3″

8¾″

roof pieces

144

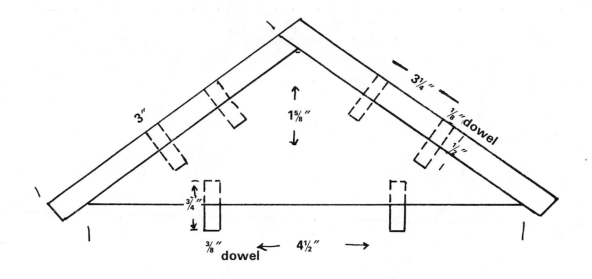

3" $1\frac{5}{8}''$ $3\frac{1}{4}''$ $\frac{1}{8}''$dowel $\frac{1}{2}''$

$\frac{3}{4}''$ $\frac{3}{8}''$ dowel $4\frac{1}{2}''$

roof cross section

To assemble the ark, glue two front and rear blocks together. Clamp until dry. Glue side pieces to blocks following diagram. Fit in bottom piece, glue, and let entire hull dry.

With coping saw, shape hull as shown. Sand smooth. Drill ⅛" blind holes for reinforcing pegs, and glue in place. Sand dowel ends when dry.

Drill 1" diameter holes in cabin parts as shown.

Glue cabin pieces into hull. When dry, glue ½" × ½" strips in bottom, ½" apart, to form slots to hold animals.

Assemble roof, butting side to side and recessed blocks to inner angle, matching recess of blocks to front and back of cabin. Drill and glue in reinforcing dowel pegs as shown. Drill blind holes in blocks, matching ones in front and back of cabin for attaching dowel pegs. Glue ⅜" diameter dowel pieces into roof blocks.

Finish, if desired, with one part white shellac and one part denatured alcohol.

Cut out animal pairs and sand edges smooth. Finish as desired.

Merry-Go-Round

The merry-go-round is built out of ½″ and ¾″ pine, dowels, and ¼″ pine for animals. A 2″ diameter wooden ball forms the top. Cut all parts beforehand for ease of assembly. You'll need:

1 dowel, ¼″ diameter, cut into eight 6″ long pieces
1 circle, 8¼″ diameter, cut from ¾″ pine
1 circle, 7″ diameter, cut from ½″ pine
1 circle, 6½″ diameter, cut from ½″ pine
1 dowel, ⅜″ diameter, 8⅜″ long
1 circle, 1½″ diameter, cut from ¾″ pine
4 pieces of ¼″ pine, 2¾″ × 3¾″ for animals

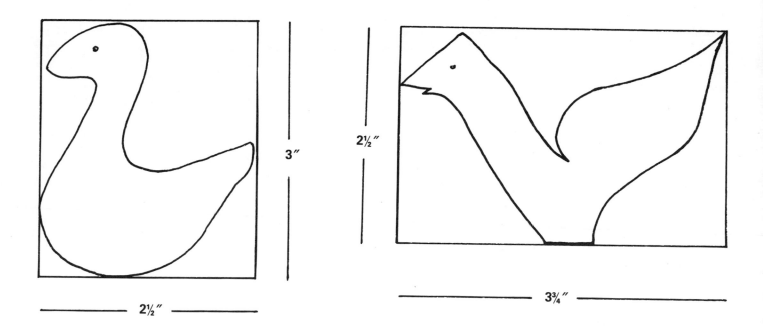

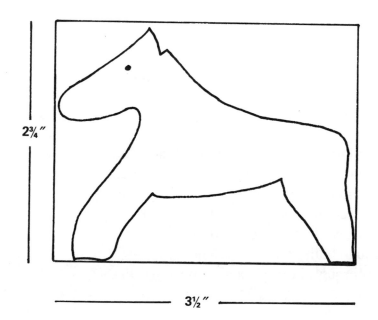

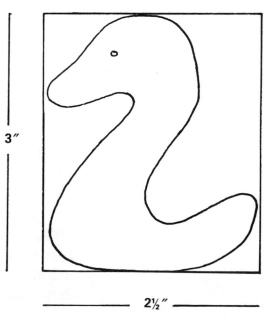

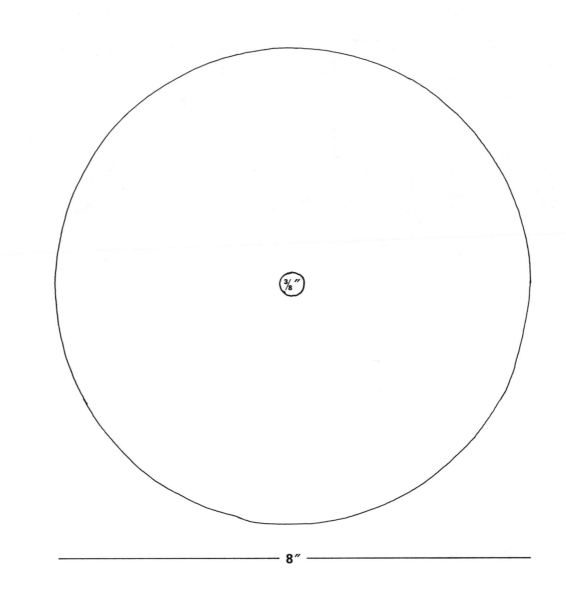

8″

Drill centered ⅜″ diameter hole in largest circle. Glue ⅜″ diameter dowel into hole and let dry. After drilling centered clearance hole one size larger than the dowel, slip 1½″ circle onto dowel rod in large circle to form the base.

Clamp 7″ and 6½″ circle together and drill centered clearance holes through both at one time. Then, drill eight holes for ¼″ dowel through both circles at once, so that they match.

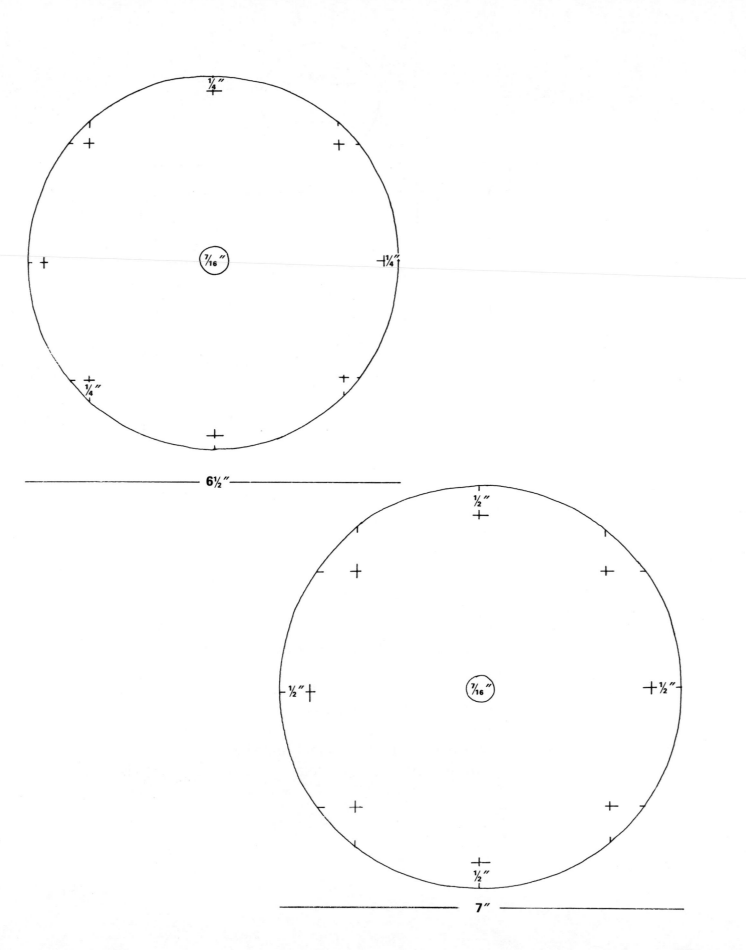

151

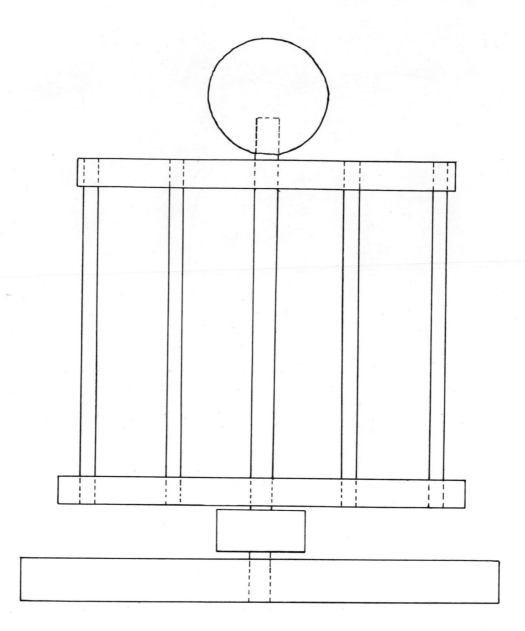

Glue side dowels into holes following photograph. Let dry.

Copy patterns for animals and cut from pieces of ¼″ pine. Follow photograph to glue one animal on each set of side dowels and let dry.

Slip merry-go-round assembly onto base dowel.

Drill a blind hole ⅜″ in diameter into the 2″ wooden ball, and glue ball to top of dowel rod. Let dry. Finish as desired.

Tiny Village with Playboard

This tiny village is built with small amounts of ¾" pine. You can make as many houses as you like with just a few feet of wood. The playboard is a sheet of ½" plywood with acrylic painted streets, trees, and bushes. You can use any size or thickness of plywood for the playboard, designing the street layout as desired.

To make the houses, use a miter box to cut the angled roof parts. Molding, which comes in many different shapes, can also be used if you can find an appropriately angled piece.

All houses are constructed in two parts, which are cut to the dimensions shown and then glued together. They can be clamped for a stronger attachment. Additional pieces, which add interest to the basic houses, can be used as you please.

To make the houses shown, use the parts given and glue together, following diagram and photograph.

For Basic House:

2 pieces, ¾″ × ¾″ × 1¼″ × 2″

For House with Dormer:

2 pieces, ¾″ × ¾″ × 1¼″ × 2″

1 piece, ⅜″ × ⅜″ × ⅜″ × 1½″ for dormer

For Long House:

2 pieces, ¾″ × ¼″ × ¾″ × 2″

For House with Attached Shed:

2 pieces, ¾″ × ¾″ × 1¼″ × 1¼″

2 pieces, ¾″ × ¾″ × ⅜″ × ¼″

For Chalet:

2 pieces, ¾″ × ⅝″ × ⅝″

2 pieces, ¾″ × 1½″ × ¼″

For Small House:

2 pieces, ¾″ × 1¼″ × ¼″

For House with a Small Extension:

2 pieces, ¾″ × ¾″ × 1¼″

1 piece, ¾″ × ¾″ × ¼″

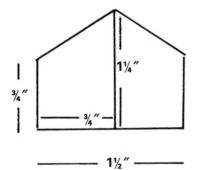

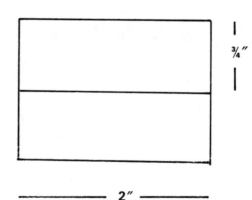

basic house

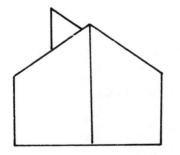

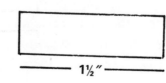

house with dormer

154

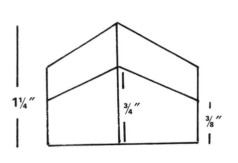

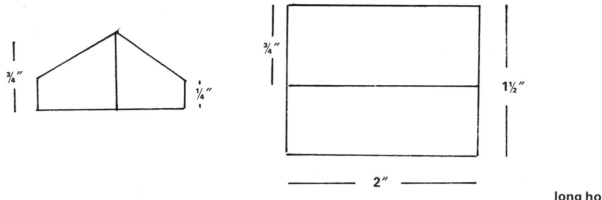

long house

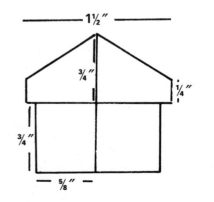

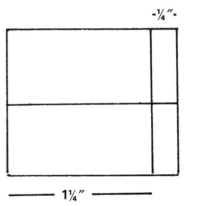

house with attached shed

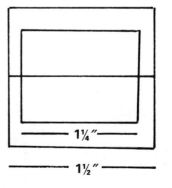

chalet

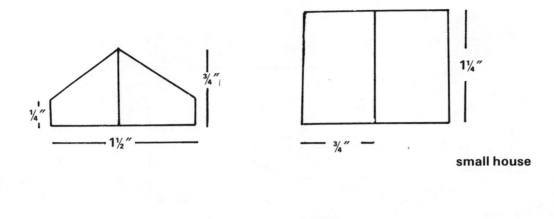

small house

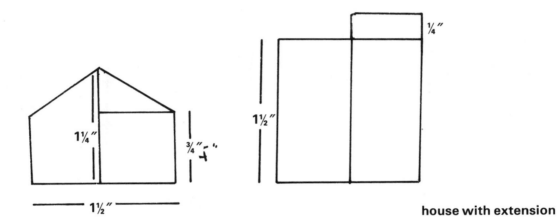

house with extension

When houses are completely dry, sand all cut edges smooth. The water tower and lamppost are made out of small wheels and short lengths of dowel. You can add different houses or vary the basic design to make various sizes. (Due to the small size of finished houses, this tiny village is best for children who are three years or older.)

Catamaran Sailboat

You can build the catamaran sailboat out of odd pieces of wood and dowels of assorted thicknesses. You'll also need a 1″ diameter wooden ball and a small piece of fabric for the sail. To build the sailboat, cut pieces as follows:

2 pieces of ¾″ diameter dowel, 6″ long, for pontoons
1 piece of pine, ¼″ × 2¾″ × 4½″, for platform
1 piece of wood, ½″ × ¾″ × 4½″, for centerpiece
2 lengths of ¼″ diameter dowel, 4″ long, for crossbars
1 length of ¼″ diameter dowel, 8¼″ long, for mast
1 piece of ¼″ diameter dowel, 3½″ long
2 pieces of ¼″ diameter dowel, 2″ long
1 piece of wood, ¼″ × ¾″ × ¾″, for top of mast
1 piece of pine, ½″ × 1½″ × 1¾″, for rudder

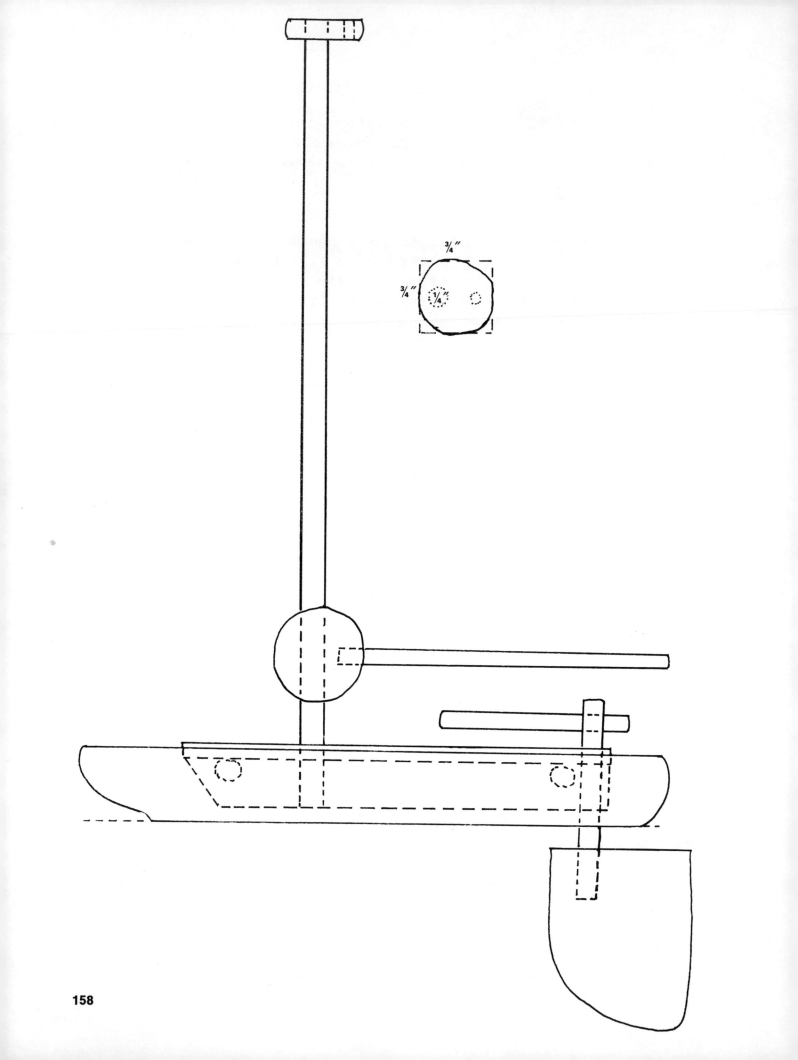

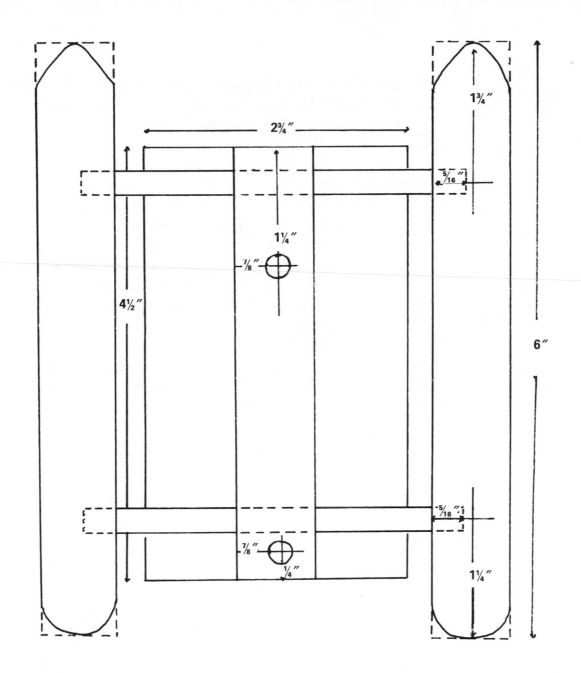

Form the shape shown at ends of pontoon dowels with sandpaper and with surform, if you have one.

Drill blind holes as indicated in pontoon sides to fit crossbars and glue pontoons and crossbars together. Let dry.

Clamp centerpiece to a piece of scrap wood and drill with ½" diameter bit at meeting to form two channels to hold centerpiece firmly on crossbars where shown by dotted lines on bottom view. Glue centerpiece channels to dowels and let dry.

Turn over assembly and glue platform on dowel cross-bars. When dry, drill holes as shown through platform and centerpiece to fit mast and clearance hole for rudder dowel.

Glue mast in place. Drill clearance hole through 1″ diameter ball for mast, drill one blind hole for boom, and glue boom dowel into ball. When dry, slip ball on mast.

Drill holes in top piece, one to fit mast and one small one to tie on sail. Glue to mast.

Cut and shape rudder as shown. Drill and glue in dowel. Insert dowel into back hole in boat and glue on a crossing dowel piece, as shown, to turn rudder.

Make a sail out of a small piece of fabric, with a ½″ casing at bottom for the boom and a folded point making a loop at top. After slipping casing over boom, tie top of sail with a short length of natural-hued string or stout thread to hole in top mast piece.

Barn and Silo

Barn and silo are made out of pine and a thick dowel. The animals are made out of short lengths of doweling, ½″, ¼″, ⅜″, ⅛″, drilled and glued together. Added details are tiny nails and bits of wire bent into shape to form horns and such. You'll need:

For Barn:
    2 pieces of pine, ⅛″ × 2½″ × 4″, for front and back
    2 sides, ⅛″ × 2⅜″ × 4½″
    2 roof bottom pieces, ⅛″ × 1⅛″ × 4½″
    2 roof top pieces, ⅛″ × 1″ × 4½″

Cut out parts and sand lightly. Assemble barn, butting and gluing sides to front and back. Hold with rubber

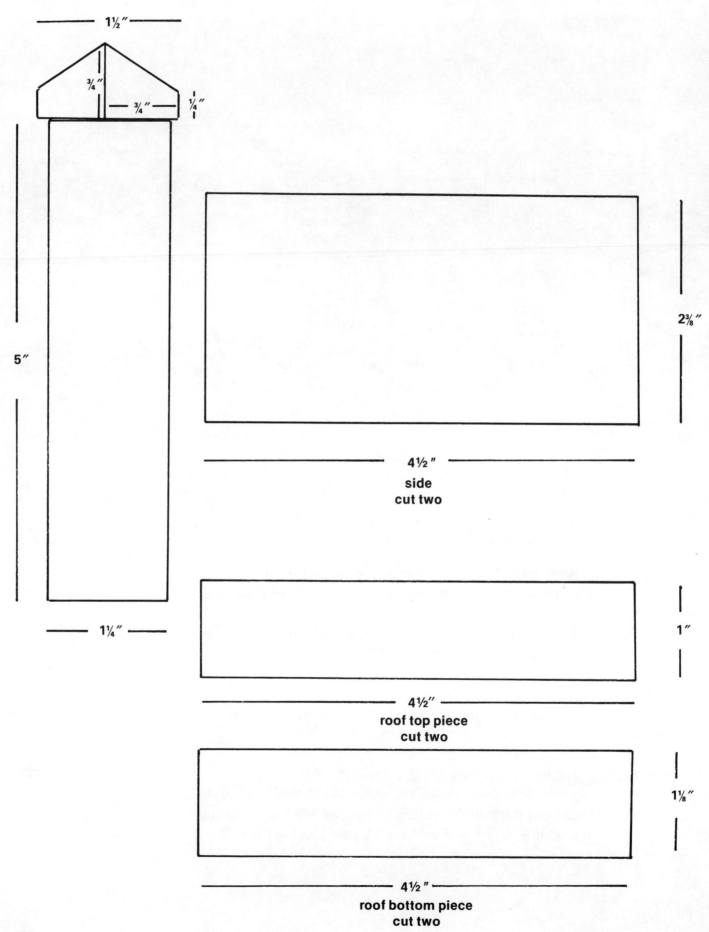

1½″

¾″

¾″

¼″

5″

1¼″

2⅜″

4½″

side
cut two

1″

4½″

roof top piece
cut two

1⅛″

4½″

roof bottom piece
cut two

162

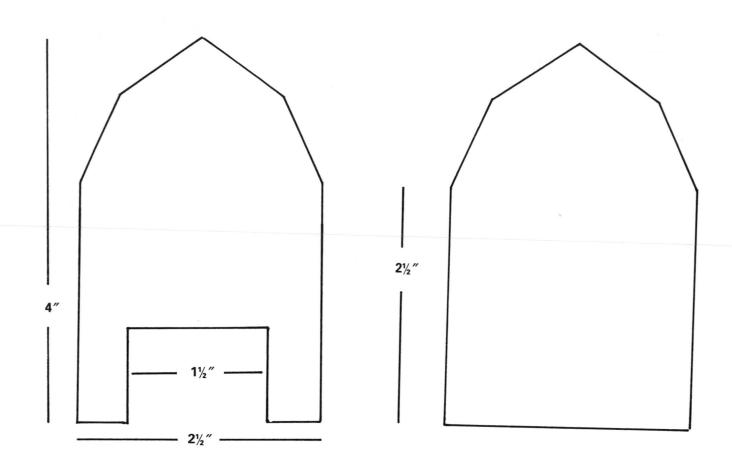

bands until dry. Then glue on roof, overlapping pieces following photograph. Hold until dry as before.

For Silo:
  1 dowel, 1¼″ diameter, 5″ long
  2 pieces, glued as for the basic house in the Tiny Village, to form a top ¼″ × ¾″ × ¾″ × 1½″

Cut the dowel to length. Build top and glue to dowel.

To make animals, follow the photograph. Using assorted dowel pieces and matching blind holes to fit dowels, you can create all kinds of animals by gluing dowels into holes.

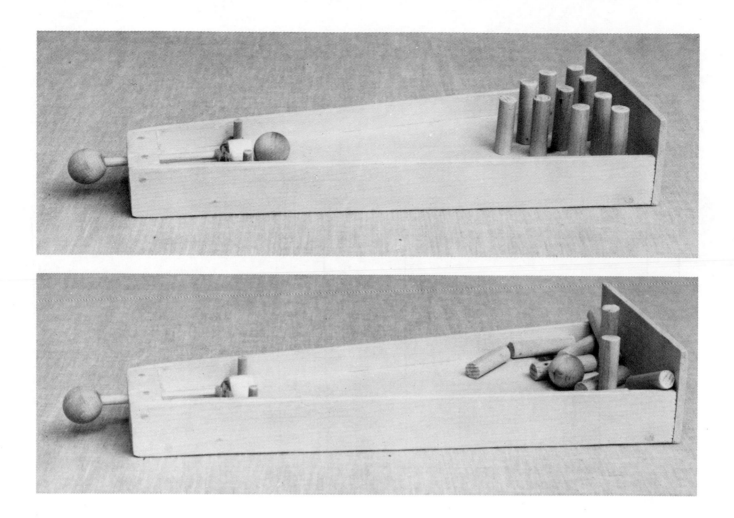

Pinball Bowling

This pinball bowling set is a variation of the traditional game of ninepins. You can make it with small amounts of pine, dowels, and two 1″ diameter wooden balls. You'll also need a couple of rubber bands. To make the bowling set, you'll need:

1 bottom piece, ¾″ × 2″ × 6″ × 14″, cut to that shape following diagram
1 piece, ¼″ × 2¾″ × 6½″, for back
2 pieces, ¼″ × 1½″ × 14″, for sides
2 pieces, ¾″ × 2½″ × 3″, cut to shape for front
1 dowel, ½″ diameter, ¾″ long

1 dowel, ¼″ diameter, 4½″ long
2 dowels, ¼″ diameter, 1″ long
2 dowels, ⅛″ diameter. 1¼″ long
9 dowels, ½″ diameter, 1¾″ long, for pins
1 dowel, ¾″ diameter, ¾″ long

Cut and sand parts. Drill ⁹⁄₃₂″ clearance hole for striker
dowel in one of the two matching front pieces as shown in
detail. Clamp and glue two front pieces together with hole
piece on top.

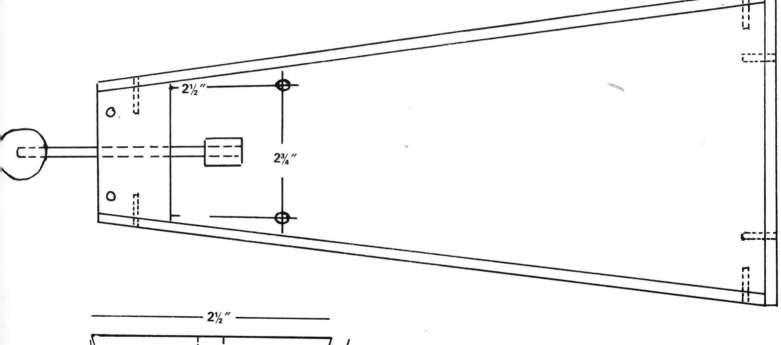

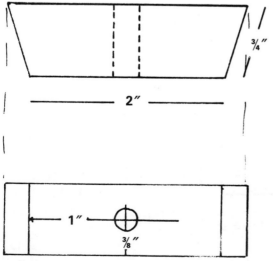

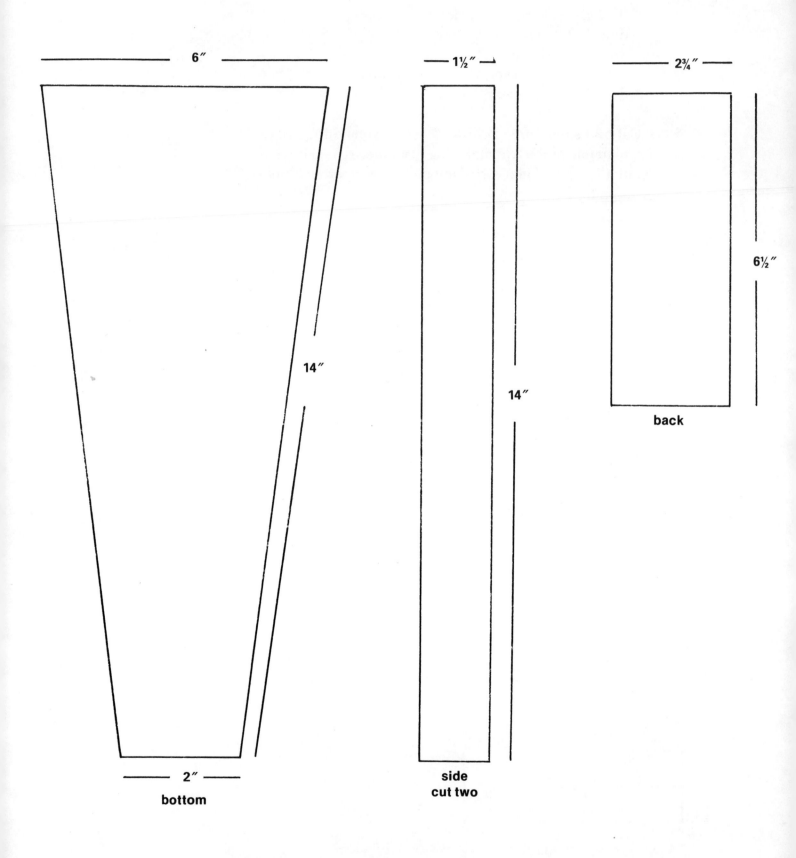

6″

14″

2″

bottom

1½″

14″

**side
cut two**

2¾″

6½″

back

166

Assemble sides, front, bottom, and back with glue. When dry, drill and glue in reinforcing dowel pegs following diagram. In bottom, drill holes to fit two 1¼" lengths of dowel; holes are ¼" diameter, ½" deep. Glue dowels in place and let dry.

Drill ¼" diameter, ¼" deep hole in one ball and glue in 4½" length of ½" dowel for striker rod. When dry, insert in hole in top front piece and drill ½" deep hole in ¾" dowel to fit ¼" striker dowel. Glue ¾" length of dowel in place at end of rod. Attach rubber bands to upright dowels following photograph.

Dump Truck

This sturdy dump truck has a swinging back gate and movable dumper unit. It is made out of clear pine, in the following lengths:

1 length of 2 × 4, 7″ long, for body
2 lengths, ½″ × 2″ × 4½″, for sides
1 length, ½″ × 1½″ × 4½″, for bottom of dumper
1 length, ½″ × 2″ × 2½″, for front of dumper
2 dowels, ¼″ diameter, 2½″ long, for wheel axles
3 dowels, ³⁄₁₆″ diameter, ¾″ long, for back gate (2 used and 1 for holding peg)
4 wheels, 2″ diameter
1 piece, ½″ × ¾″ × 1½″, for hinge swivel block

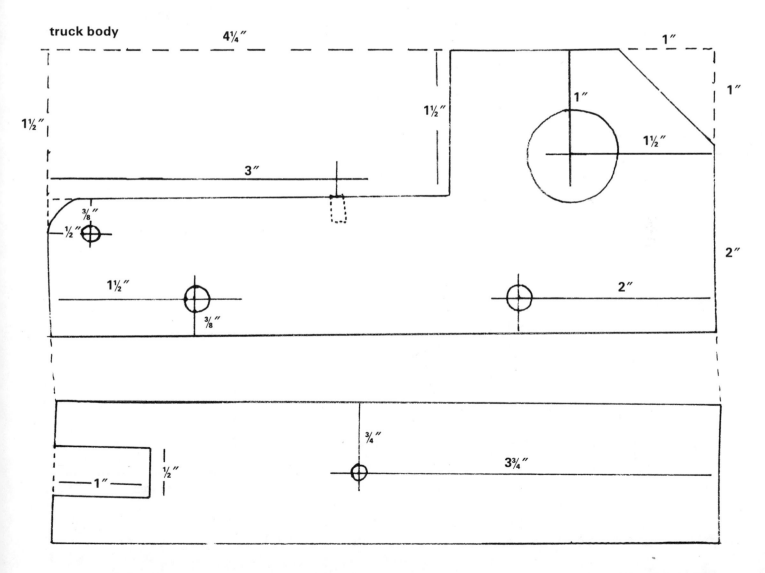

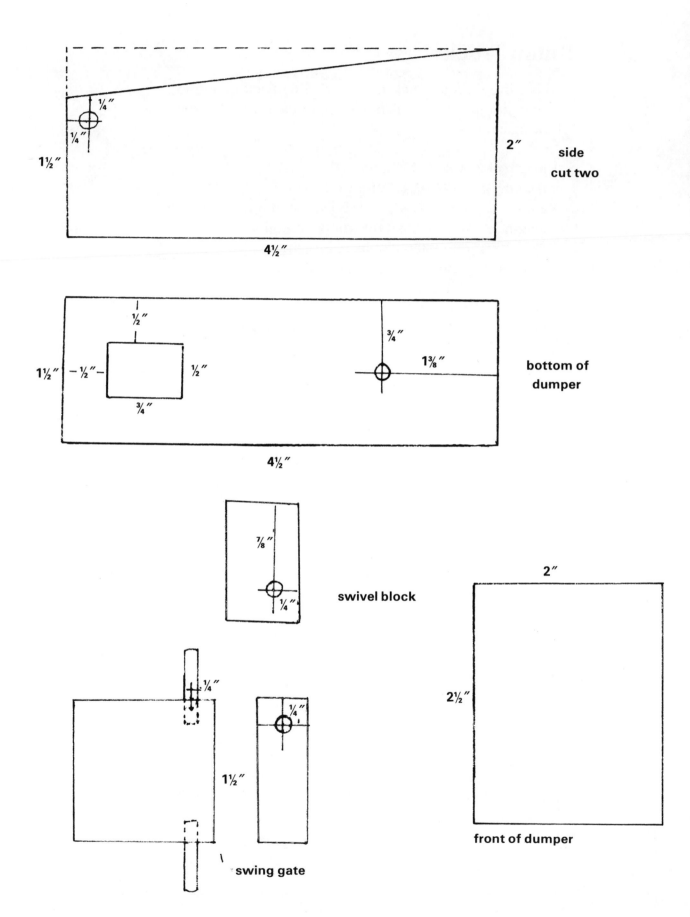

¼″

¼″

1½″

2″

side
cut two

4½″

½″

1½″ — ½″ — ½″

¾″ 1⅜″

¾″

bottom of
dumper

4½″

⅞″

¼″

swivel block

2″

2½″

¼″

¼″

1½″

swing gate

front of dumper

170

Cut and sand parts, following diagram for cutting to above dimensions. Drill holes in parts as shown, making clearance holes into sides for dowels at sides of swing gate, at top of swivel hinge block for attaching dowel; drill axle holes in body and blind clearance hole in body to receive holding dowel in bottom of dumper.

Cut ½" × ¾" hole in bottom of dumper as shown.

Assemble dumper with glue. (Leave one side off until gate is in place.) Glue swivel block into hole in bottom so that hole through block extends below. Drill blind hole to fit and glue in holding dowel as indicated at bottom of dumper.

Drill holes to fit dowels at side of swing gate and matching holes in sides of dumper. The holes in sides are clearance holes, which allow gate to swing. Position gate in back of dumper and glue dowels in place in gate. Place gate in one side and glue other side in place. Let dry. Glue wheels to axles and attach in usual manner.

To hold dumper to truck body, place dowel through truck body and swivel block, following photograph. Glue in place. Let dry. Finish as desired.

Steam Tractor

The steam tractor has swiveling front wheels and a smokestack. You can build it out of short lengths of pine, dowels, and wheels. You can also cut out the wheels with a circle cutter and drill centered holes to fit axles. To make the tractor, you'll need:

1 piece, ½″ × 1½″ × 2¾″, for roof
1 piece, 1½″ × 2″ × 2¾″, for body
1 piece, 1″ × 1½″ × 3½″, for engine, cut to shape following diagram
4 dowels, ¼″ diameter, 1¾″ long, for roof pegs
1 dowel, ¼″ diameter, 1″ long, for body peg
2 wheels, 2¼″ diameter, 1½″ thick
1 dowel, ¼″, 6″ long, for back axle
1 dowel, ¾″ diameter, 1⅛″ long, for smokestack
1 piece, ¾″ × ¾″ × ½″, for front wheel block
1 dowel, ¼″ diameter, 2″ long, for front steering dowel
1 dowel, ³⁄₁₆″ diameter, 1¼″ long, for front axle
2 front wheels, 1″ diameter, ⅜″ thick

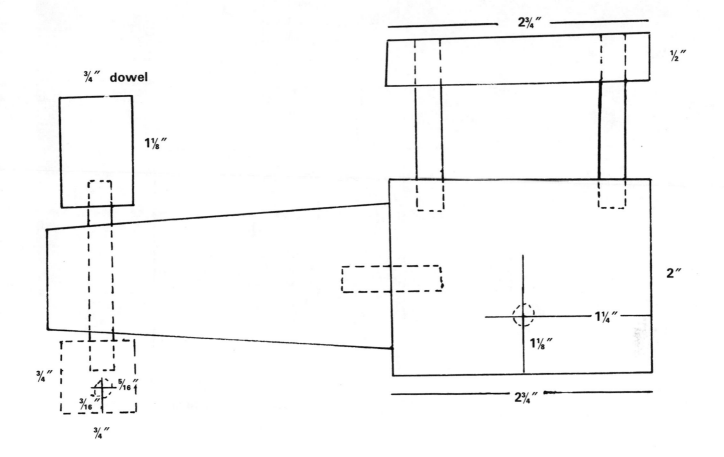

¾″ dowel

1⅛″

¾″

⁵⁄₁₆″

³⁄₁₆″

¾″

2¾″

½″

2″

1¼″

1⅛″

2¾″

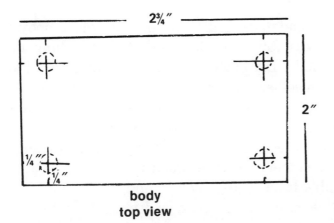

2¾″

2″

¼″

¼″

**body
top view**

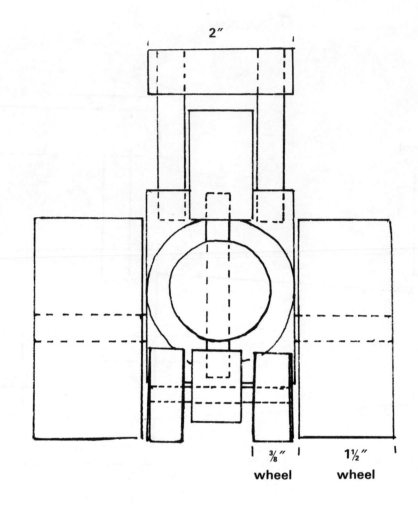

Cut and sand parts. Drill %₁₆″ clearance hole in body and engine pieces following diagram. Drill matching blind holes in body and engine pieces for reinforcing dowel; glue parts together with dowel in place. Let dry.

Drill holes as shown and assemble roof with dowel bars. Drill holes for and glue roof bars into body piece.

Glue one wheel to rear axle, insert in drilled axle hole and glue on other rear wheel. Let dry.

Assemble front wheels, dowel, and insert in clearance holes. Glue on smokestack and let dry.

Finish as desired.

Balancing Dancer

Balancing dancer spins on top of its dowel column without losing its step. You can make it with small amounts of wood and doweling. You'll also need some heavy wire and two 1-ounce fishing weights. To make it, you'll need:

1 length of 12″ pine lattice, ¼″ × 1⅜″
1 dowel, 1″ diameter, 6″ long, for column
1 piece of pine, ¾″ × 3″ × 3″, for base
1 dowel, ¼″ diameter, 1″ long, for hand rod
1 dowel, ⅛″ diameter, 1½″ long, for attaching peg

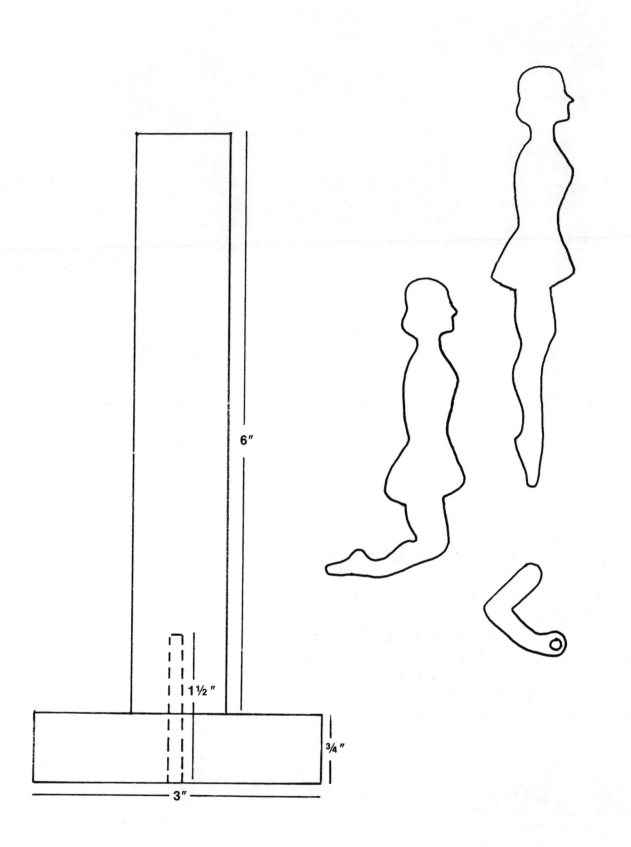

6″

1½″

¾″

3″

Cut out two pieces for arms, and two body pieces following diagram. Glue body pieces together. Drill $\frac{3}{16}''$ hole lengthwise through 1″ length of $\frac{1}{4}''$ dowel. Insert through hands and glue in place, trimming end as needed to fit. While glue for hands is still tacky, glue arms to body. Straighten hands on dowel if necessary.

Drill and attach dowel column to base, with reinforcing length of $\frac{1}{8}''$ dowel, as indicated.

Thread wire through hands and dowel, bend to shape, and trim to length shown. Tie or solder weights to ends of wire.

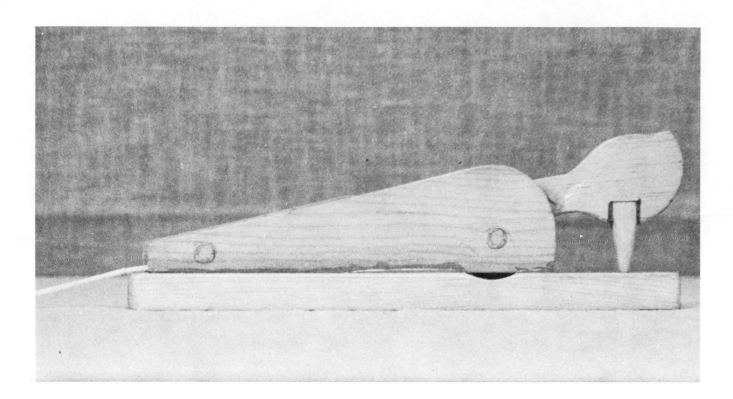

Woodpecker

The woodpecker is made out of the following pieces:

2 wings, ⅛″ thick, 1¾″ × 5½″, cut to shape
1 body and head, ¼″ thick, 1½″ × 5½″, cut to shape
2 head pieces, ⅛″ thick, 1¾″ × 1½″, cut to shape
1 dowel, ¼″ diameter, 1¼″ long
1 piece of wood, ¼″ × ¾″ × ¾″
1 mounting board, 1½″ thick, 8″ × 2″
2 wheels, ⅝″ diameter, ¼″ thick
small ball of thin cord

Cut and sand pieces. Glue head pieces to either side of head on body piece; drill ⅛″ hole in bottom.

Drill ¼″ diameter holes at top of wings as shown. Then drill a ⅜″ hole in bottom.

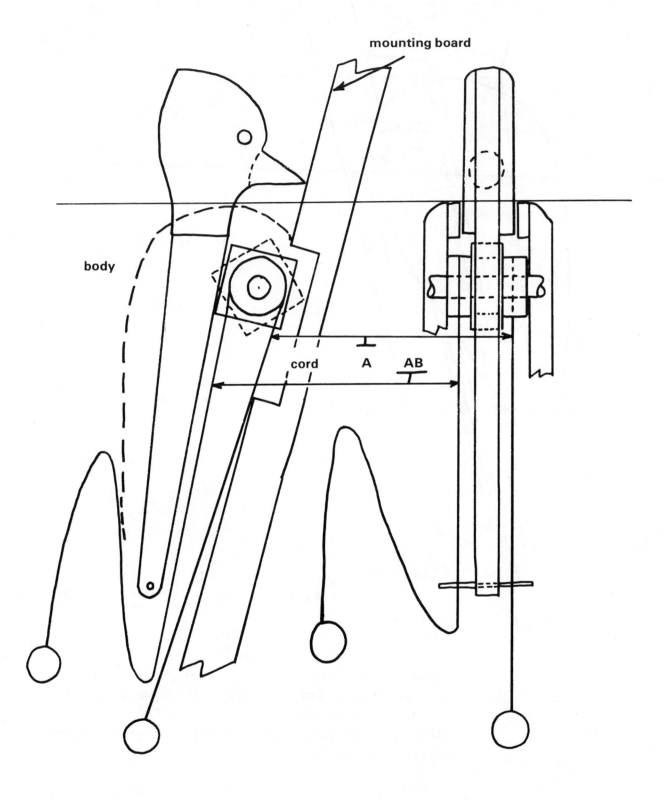

mounting board

body

cord   A   AB

Glue the ¾″ square in center of the ¼″ dowel. Insert dowel into wheel, placing one wheel on each side; glue in place.

Glue the dowel to the holes in the wings.

Glue wings to mounting board.

Place body between wings and insert ⅛″ dowel through ⅜″ holes in wings and ⅛″ hole in body. Glue in place in body holes.

Cut a 24″ length of cord and wrap center around wheels. Pull cord and the woodpecker pecks.

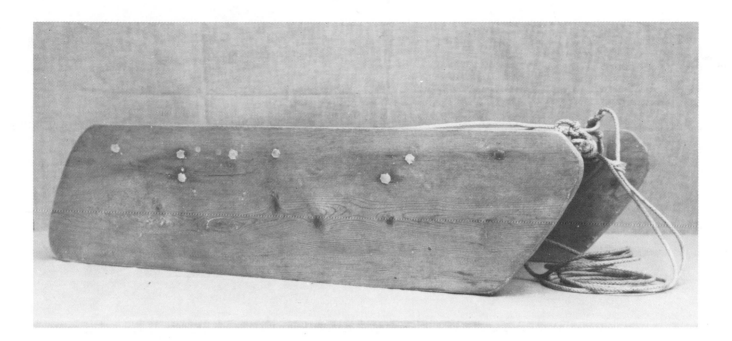

Sled

To build this full-sized pull-along sled, you'll need:

2 lengths of pine, 1½″ × 9½″, 3′ long, for sides
1 length of pine, 1½″ × 13½″, 3′ long (or 1 piece of ¾″
    plywood, 14″ × 27″), for platform
1 length of pine, 1½″ × 1½″, 6′ long, for cleats
1 dowel, ¼″ diameter
thin rope

Cut two side pieces to shape following pattern shown.
Sand smooth.

Cut 3′ length for platform to 27″ long or use plywood as
given above.

Cut 1½″ × 1½″ length of pine into two 27″ lengths for
cleats.

Drill two ¾″ holes in front of platform where shown for
pull cords.

Assemble with waterproof glue, butting sides to plat-

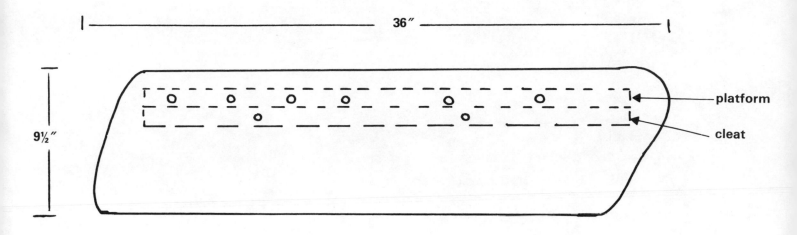

36″

9½″

platform

cleat

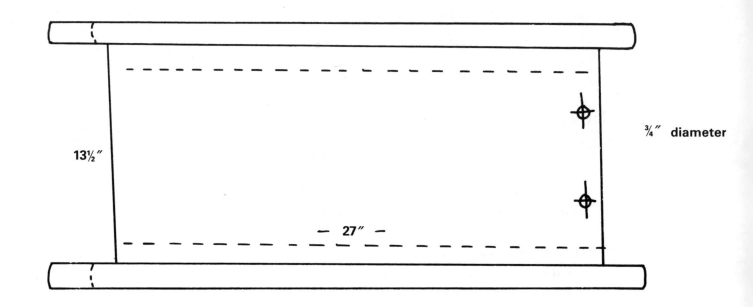

13½″

27″

¾″ diameter

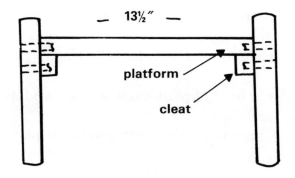

13½″

platform

cleat

form, placing platform 1″ down from top edges of sides. Place and glue two full-length cleats at underside of joint.

Drill ¼″ diameter holes and insert 2″ long dowel pegs to strengthen attachment of platform and cleats to sides.

Cut two lengths of rope, one for child to hold, and a longer one for adult to pull. Tie both ends of both lengths into holes in platform.

Finish as desired.

Wax bottoms of runners with parafin or other wax before each use.

Appendix: Sources of Supplies

When you want to find a specific tool, an unusual wood, or just to browse through what's available, and you don't have a local supplier, you can look at the catalogs of mail-order suppliers. The catalogs are usually interesting and often informative as well. The following companies are among these sources. You can send for their catalogs, often for a small charge which may be refundable with an order. This list is for your convenience, but does not constitute an endorsement.

Robert M. Albrecht 8635 Yolanda Avenue Northridge, CA 91324	Unusual woods, tools, glue
Alnap Corp. 66 Reade Street New York, NY 10007	Tools
American Machine and Tool Royersford, PA 19468	Tools
Bedford Lumber Co. Box 65 Shelbyville, TN 37160	Woods

Brookstone Co. 126 Vose Farm Road Peterborough, NH 03458	Tools, glue, accessories
Chicago Wheel and Manufacturing 1101 Monroe Street Chicago, IL 60607	Tools
Albert Constantine & Son 2050 Eastchester Road Bronx, NY 10461	Woods, tools, glue
The Craftool Co. 2323 Reach Road Williamsport, PA 17701	Woods, tools
Craftsman Wood Service 2727 South Mary Street Chicago, IL 60608	Woods, tools, glue
Educational Lumber Co. Box 5373, Meadow Road Asheville, NC 28803	Woods
John Harra Wood Co. 39 West 19 Street New York, NY 10011	Unusual Woods
Johnson Wood Products Route 1 Strawberry Point, IA 52076	Woods
Love Built Toys and Crafts 2907 Lake Forest Road Box 5459 Tahoe City, CA 95730	Wooden wheels, accessories
M & M Hardwood 5344 Vineland Street North Hollywood, CA 91601	Woods, tools

Sierra Wood Design   Rare woods
Box 320
El Portal, CA 95318

Triarco Arts and Crafts   Power tools
7330 North Clark Street
Chicago, IL 60620

Woodcraft Supply Co.   Woods, tools, accessories
313 Montvale Avenue
Woburn, MA 01801

Woodstream Arts   Hardwoods
Box 11471
Knox, TN 37919

Index